Ke[illegible] en you

V[illegible] foot, you will enjoy[illegible] journey back in time. Compare the York of old with what you can see today —revisit the old stone gates and city walls as they once were; tour the ancient Minster; wander the streets and alleyways of the city and inspect the fine old buildings; see the monuments and antiquities as our ancestors saw them. Examine the many alterations to York that have taken place during our lives, and which we may have taken for granted.

At the turn of a page you will gain fascinating insights into York's unique history.

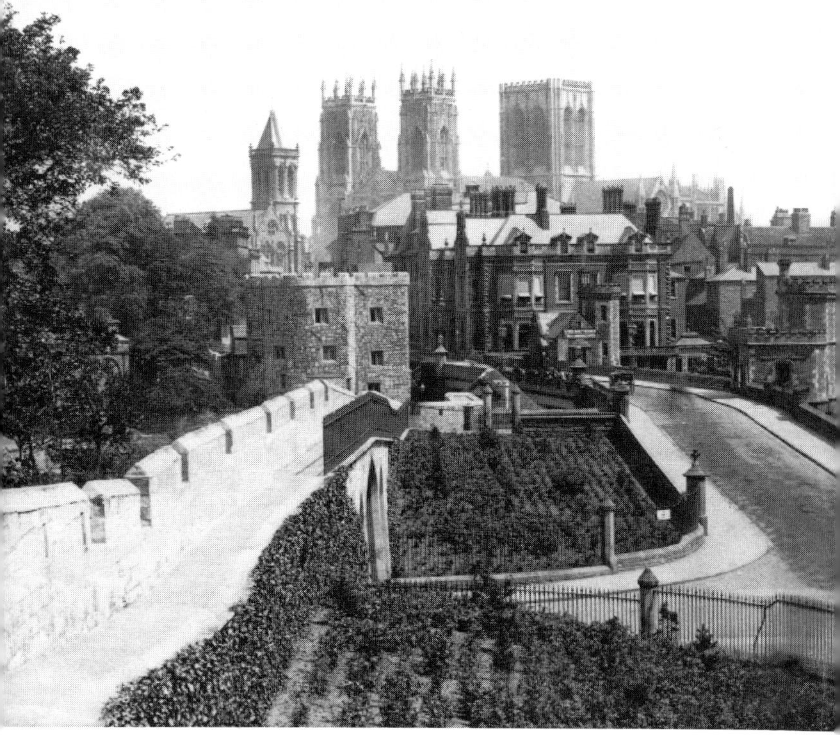

FRANCIS FRITH'S

pocket ALBUM

YORK

A POCKET ALBUM

Adapted from an original book by
Maureen Anderson

First published in the United Kingdom in 2004 by
Frith Book Company Ltd

ISBN 1-85937-871-4

British Library Cataloguing in Publication Data

York—A Pocket Album
Adapted from an original book by Maureen Anderson

Frith Book Company Ltd
Frith's Barn, Teffont,
Salisbury, Wiltshire SP3 5QP
Tel: +44 (0) 1722 716 376
Email: info@francisfrith.co.uk
www.francisfrith.co.uk

Printed and bound in Great Britain by MPG, Bodmin

Front Cover: CONEY STREET 1909 / 61723

The colour-tinting is for illustrative purposes only, and is not intended to be historically accurate.

Frontispiece: YORK, from City Walls 1885 18429

AS WITH ANY HISTORICAL DATABASE THE FRITH ARCHIVE IS CONSTANTLY BEING CORRECTED AND IMPROVED AND THE PUBLISHERS WOULD WELCOME INFORMATION ON OMISSIONS OR INACCURACIES

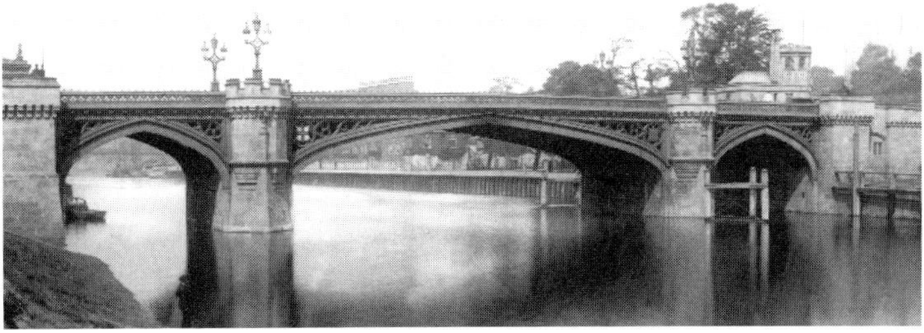

CONTENTS

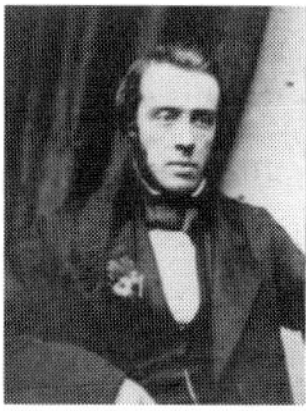

FRANCIS FRITH

VICTORIAN PIONEER

Francis Frith, founder of the world-famous photographic archive, was a complex and multi-talented man. A devout Quaker and a highly successful Victorian businessman, he was philosophical by nature and pioneering in outlook. By 1855 he had already established a wholesale grocery business in Liverpool, and sold it for the astonishing sum of £200,000, which is the equivalent today of over £15,000,000.Now in his thirties, and captivated by the new science of photography, Frith set out on a series of pioneering journeys up the Nile and to the Near East.

INTRIGUE AND EXPLORATION

He was the first photographer to venture beyond the sixth cataract of the Nile. Africa was still the mysterious 'Dark Continent', and Stanley and Livingstone's historic meeting was a decade into the future. The conditions for picture taking confound belief. He laboured for hours in his wicker dark-room in the sweltering heat of the desert, while the volatile chemicals fizzed dangerously in their trays. Back in London he exhibited his photographs and was 'rapturously cheered' by members of the Royal Society. His reputation as a photographer was made overnight.

VENTURE OF A LIFE-TIME

By the 1870s the railways had threaded their way across the country, and Bank Holidays and half-day Saturdays had been made obligatory by Act of Parliament. All of a sudden the working man and his family were able to enjoy days out, take holidays, and see a little more of the world.

With typical business acumen, Francis Frith foresaw that these new tourists would enjoy having souvenirs to commemorate their days out. For the next thirty years he travelled the country by train and by pony and trap, producing fine photographs of seaside resorts and beauty spots that were keenly bought by millions of Victorians. These prints were painstakingly pasted into family albums and pored over during the dark nights of winter, rekindling precious memories of summer excursions. Frith's studio was soon supplying retail shops all over the country, and by 1890 F Frith & Co had become the greatest specialist photographic publishing company in the world, with over 2,000 sales outlets, and pioneered the picture postcard.

FRANCIS FRITH'S LEGACY

Francis Frith had died in 1898 at his villa in Cannes, his great project still growing. The archive he created continued in business for another seventy years. By 1970 it contained over a third of a million pictures showing 7,000 British towns and villages.

Frith's legacy to us today is of immense significance and value, for the magnificent archive of evocative photographs he created provides a unique record of change in the cities, towns and villages throughout Britain over a century and more. Frith and his fellow studio photographers revisited locations many times down the years to update their views, compiling for us an enthralling and colourful pageant of British life and character.

We are fortunate that Frith was dedicated to recording the minutiae of everyday life. For it is this sheer wealth of visual data, the painstaking chronicle of changes in dress, transport, street layouts, buildings, housing, engineering and landscape that captivates us so much today, offering us a powerful link with the past and with the lives of our ancestors.

Computers have now made it possible for Frith's many thousands of images to be accessed almost instantly. The archive offers every one of us an opportunity to examine the places where we and our families have lived and worked down the years. Its images, depicting our shared past, are now bringing pleasure and enlightenment to millions around the world a century and more after his death.

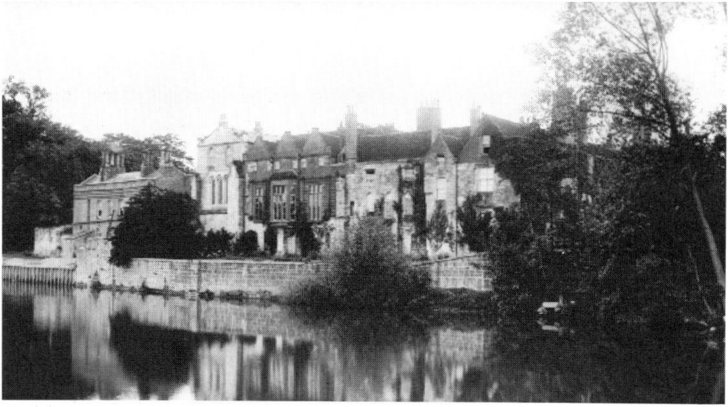

BISHOPTHORPE PALACE FROM THE RIVER 1893 32044

YORK
AN INTRODUCTION

YORK IS JUST less than 220 miles from London, and is located within the boundaries of North Yorkshire in the beautiful Vale of York. The population is 177,350 - a portion of this is made up of the student body that attend the relatively new university. Much of the surrounding area is still very much agricultural; a substantial amount of the economy derives from the food industry as well as from tourism. Once an encampment, and originally built at the confluence of the River Ouse and the River Foss, the city now spans a much wider area on both sides of the two rivers. Until the Industrial Revolution, which largely passed it by, York was once the most important town in the north of England.

In Roman times, York was the principal military base in Britain, and in the 9th century it was the capital of a Viking kingdom. Because of its importance in the scheme of things, some records have survived; these records, along with what has been excavated, have enabled historians and archaeologists to piece together a vast amount of York's past. Its rich history spans more than nineteen centuries. York began in AD71 as a Roman camp, which was home to some 6,000 soldiers. The Romans named the outpost Eboracum, which is thought to have meant 'a place of yew trees'. The location would have been chosen because the rivers would help protect it from attack; ironically, centuries later, the Vikings used the rivers as their gateway for invasion. Near the soldiers' encampment a civilian town sprang up, which was peopled by the traders and their families who supplied the soldiers with clothing, food and the things necessary to life. One Roman building that still stands is the Multiangular Tower; there is also a column that stands 30 feet high which was found during excavations to the Minster in 1969, lying where it had fallen. The York Civic Trust had it erected in the Minster Yard in 1971. A public house called the Roman Bath Inn has a floor made up of panels of glass where one can look onto the remains of a Roman bath house that was excavated in 1930.

During the Saxon period, Eboracum became known as Eoforwic. This period is the least documented, but we do know that the Saxons were instrumental in the spread of Christianity and established the foundations for many of the churches. In 866 the Vikings invaded, and changed the name of the town to Jorvik. Some of the place names, such as Micklegate and Goodramgate, are inheritances from the occupation, although the Vikings were here for less than a century. As with the Romans, not many of the buildings above ground have survived, but excavations have turned up many well-preserved artefacts. The Jorvik Viking Centre, a huge tourist attraction which brings millions of visitors every year, is built upon the site of an excavated Viking settlement, and the artefacts found here have been used in the museum. Even the Viking rubbish dumps were a treasure trove to the historians: shoes, utensils and bits of clothing that had been discarded all serve to show the Viking way of life. The impression we have formed of these people is of frightening-looking men with huge beards and horned helmets who spent their lives burning, raping and pillaging; but the excavations of their settlements show a different picture. The Jorvik Centre proves that once the Vikings put down roots in an area, they had a settled family life.

During the Norman period, in 1089, a large cathedral was built; many churches were built too, some of which have survived. The 13th century saw building begin on a new cathedral replacing the earlier edifice. The building of the present Minster was spread over a period of 250 years. Recently an enormous amount of restoration work has been carried out all over York. There are approximately 1,000 listed buildings in the city, and about twenty of these are churches. The Georgians and then the Victorians have also left their legacies in many of the wonderful buildings that still remain.

The Romans had built walls spanning nearly three miles in an almost complete circuit around their encampment; chains were stretched across the rivers where they prevented the continuation of the walls. Thus the outpost became a fortress town. The Vikings covered these walls with earth. Then, in medieval times, the walls that still stand today were built on top of the original ramparts with magnesian limestone brought from Tadcaster. The four main entrance gates still survive.

Oil lamps were used until 1824, when gas lighting was introduced to the streets. How the people must have rejoiced to be able to walk the streets in comparative brightness instead of in the murky light of the old lamps. It is said that well over a hundred ghosts can still be seen or heard in the city; the popular Ghost Walks take visitors on a tour of public houses, churches and other buildings as the sad tales behind the hauntings are told. One story is of the Towpath Ghost, a white headless lady who is said to wander up and down the Ouse towpath looking for the people who robbed and killed her while she was strolling along the riverbank. Her body lay hidden for so long that the head had separated from the body. Another story is of children crying; they were supposed to have been killed by the wicked master of a ragged school. Whether one believes in ghosts or not, in a city with such a long and sometimes quite violent history, with so many tears and so much laughter, with so many births and deaths, something must surely remain. Perhaps the spirits of the people that have lived here through the ages are impregnated into the walls and buildings.

Besides the hauntings, there are many stories of the people who made their mark on York's history, names that will never be forgotten. They include Roman soldiers and emperors, Vikings such as Eric Bloodaxe, and the dukes of York, six of whom were crowned king; more recently there was Guy Fawkes, who was born here, Dick Turpin, who spent his last days in the condemned cell of the prison, and Margaret Clitherow, who was proclaimed a saint. She was married to a butcher from the Shambles in the 16th century. Arrested for harbouring priests and refusing to plead, she was tried at what was then the Common Hall (now the Guildhall) and sentenced to death by pressing. A house in the Shambles is now set aside as a shrine to her.

Tradition still plays a key role here. At Christmas the high altar in the Minster has mistletoe placed upon it as decoration; the plant said to have magical properties and its associations are pagan, so it is unknown how this practice came to be. Displays of sword dancing are held in St Sampson's Square on Plough Monday, the first Monday after 6 January; again the origins of this custom are unknown - the dancing was once performed by farm labourers. The Mystery Plays are performed in the Minster Yard, usually by amateur groups; 'mystery' derives from the word 'mastery', and all the plays are biblical.

The pride of the city, and one of the most famous buildings in the world, is York Minster, York's cathedral, which was completed in 1472 and restored between 1967 and 1972. An enormous edifice, it boasts wonderful Gothic architecture, woodwork and stonework, and also stained glass, 128 windows in all, spanning 800 years of glass painting. One part of a medieval glass panel shows that the painter had a sense of humour - it depicts what is known as the Monkey's Funeral. Nine monkeys are pictured: the deceased is carried shoulder-high by four pallbearers, while a bell-ringer leads the procession with a cross-bearer behind. The bereaved young monkey is in the centre foreground, being comforted by a friend. Last but not least, one monkey is sampling the wine at the funeral feast. The Minster is still used for daily worship, as well as for services on important occasions.

The organ music is known world-wide. Scholars come to study the Minster's history and to use the library, and tourists flock from all over the world to wonder at its beauty.

Although the chimney stacks and the large dull grey buildings relating to heavy industry never made a serious impact on York, the sweet industry made its mark. The origins of Rowntree Mackintosh's and Terry's chocolate empires began in retail businesses in the 18th century. The businesses eventually developed into large-scale confectionery manufacture; in the late 1930s they were employing over 12,000 people. Both these firms are still major players in the confectionery and food industry today. Glass works and instrument-making were also once big business. The coming of the railway had a huge impact, and brought prosperity to many. George Hudson, dubbed 'the Railway King', was instrumental in the development of the railway and its related buildings. He was three times Lord Mayor, but eventually crooked wheeling and dealing with funds brought his downfall; for over a century his name was shunned in York. In recent years, however, his input has been recognised, and a street and a building have been named after him.

There was a long wait for a university in this city, but once plans were approved, work went ahead quite quickly. Some older historical buildings were incorporated into the structure of the plans and the first two colleges were opened in the 1960s, with others following over the next few years.

Such is the wealth of preserved history here, that days rather than hours are needed to tour this amazing city. On turning a corner, beautiful old trees, some older than the buildings, stretch their branches to the sky where you would least expect it. The ruins of St Mary's Abbey stand in the peaceful, well-manicured Museum Gardens, giving an insight of how harsh life must have been: the thick stone walls and open fires were the only protection from the cold. There is a wealth of medieval stained glass in some of the churches and in many of the buildings, as well as in the Minster. Along the snickelways, we can look above the shop fronts and see public house signs, tea shop signs, statues, carvings, gargoyles and so on –

they show what the buildings were once used for or who once lived there. As we walk along the walls, we can see breathtaking views of the rivers and the city. Many buildings that have been preserved or painstakingly restored are open to the public; some are instantly recognisable in this compilation of photographs taken more than a century ago. At dusk many of the buildings are now floodlit. Modern gift shops and cafes now line the little streets, and millions of visitors from every corner of the world tour the city every year, but that does not take anything away from the magical atmosphere - indeed, it seems instead to enhance it. Whatever we do or see here, it gives us an unforgettable experience of a journey back in time.

Just as the tides of the rivers have ebbed and flowed unrelentingly through the ages, so has the history and prosperity of this ancient city. Although the buildings from so many different eras and of differing architectural styles are side by side, somehow they all live together in perfect harmony. They give the impression that here the past merges into the present, and also that the city of York will endure to give pleasure to future generations - and also to teach them that knowing about their heritage can help to shape the future.

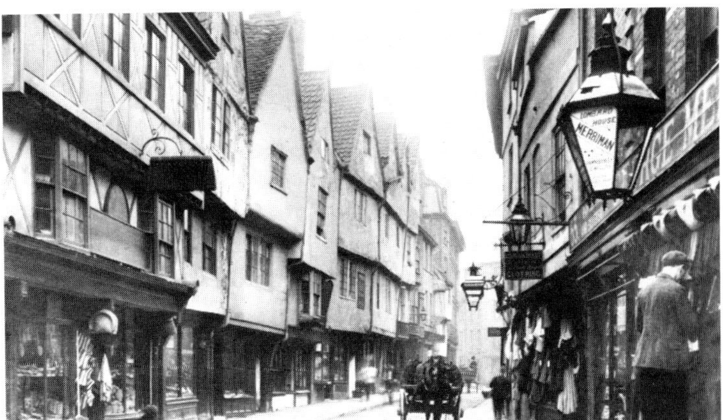

YORK, LOW PETERGATE 1892 30632

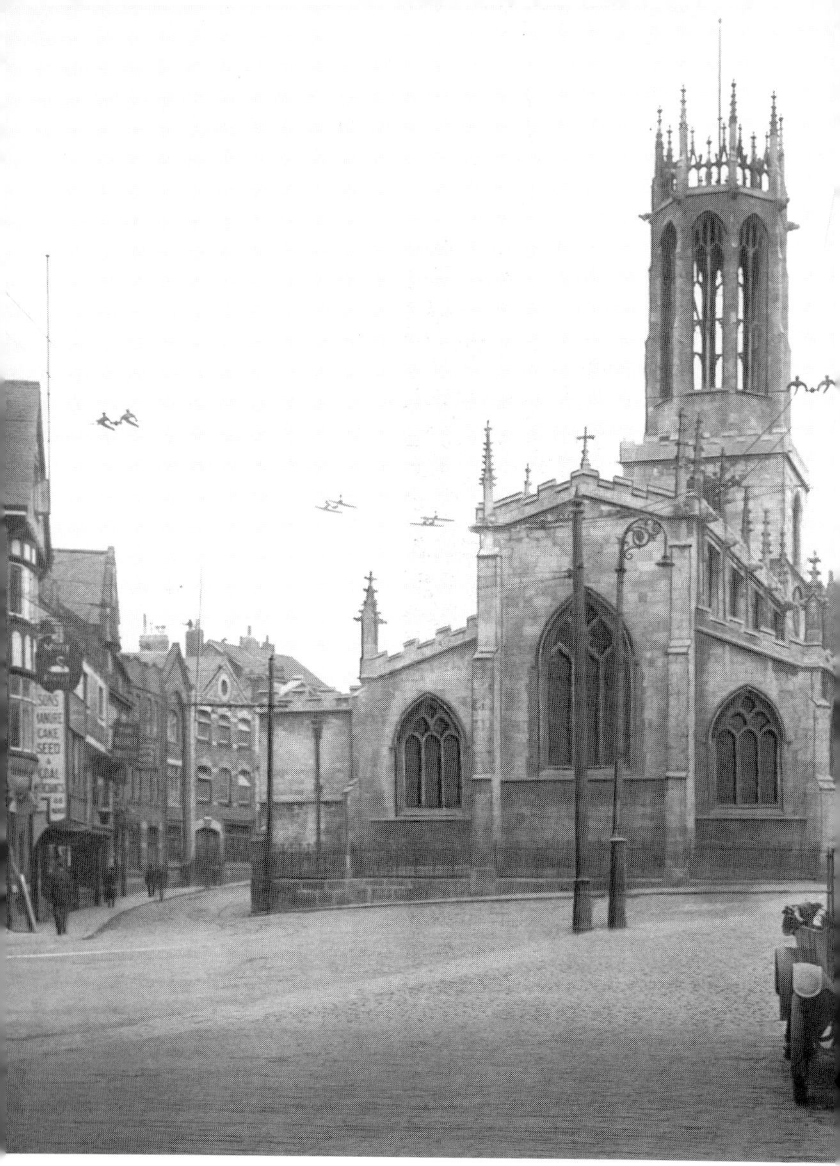
SONS
CAKE
SEED
COAL

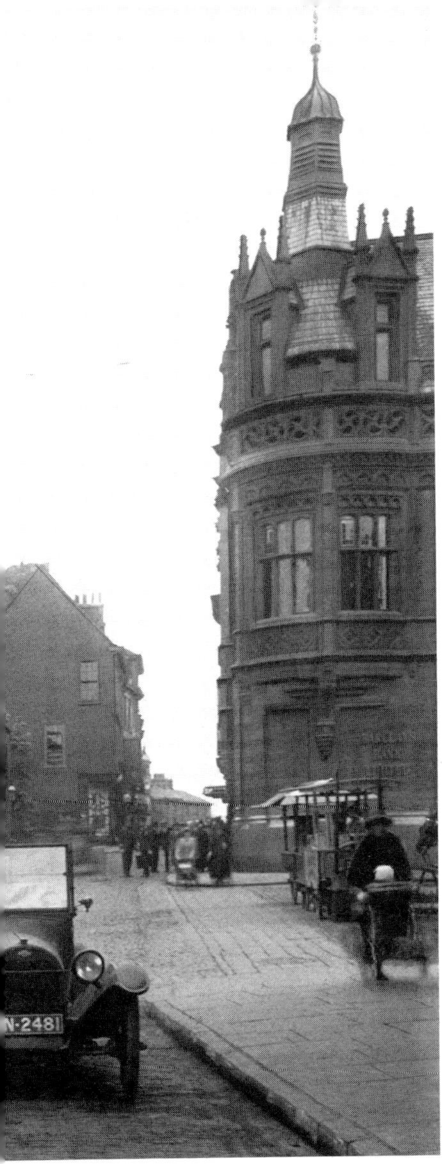

This church has a lantern tower and is said to be the resting place of 39 Lord Mayors. It is the Guild Church of York. It contains a 17th Century pulpit from which John Wesley preached.

ALL SAINTS' CHURCH, PAVEMENT

1921 / 70648

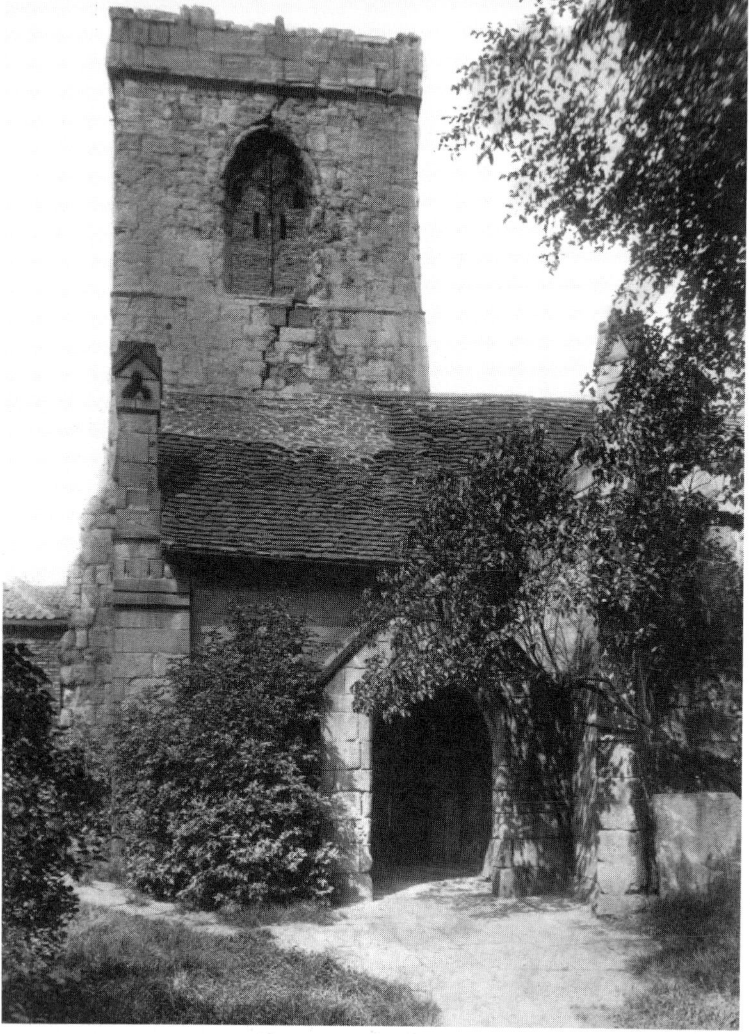

HOLY TRINITY CHURCH

GOODRAMGATE *1909 / 61857*

During the siege of York it is thought that guns were placed on the roof here, but there is some controversy about this. In about 1720 St Olave's was almost entirely rebuilt with stone from St Mary's Abbey. Adjacent to the church there was once a chapel called St-Mary-at-the-Gate, of which a small portion of the stonework still survives.

ST OLAVE'S CHURCH

MARYGATE *c1885* / 18480

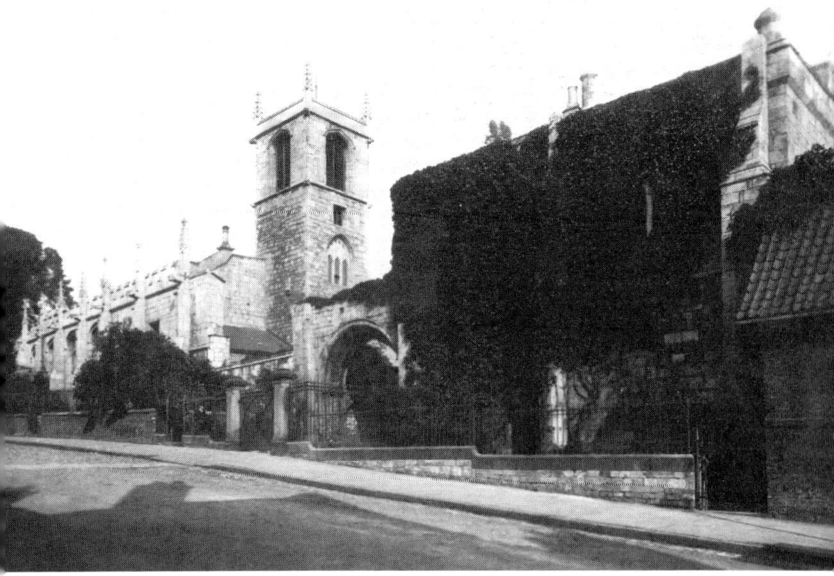

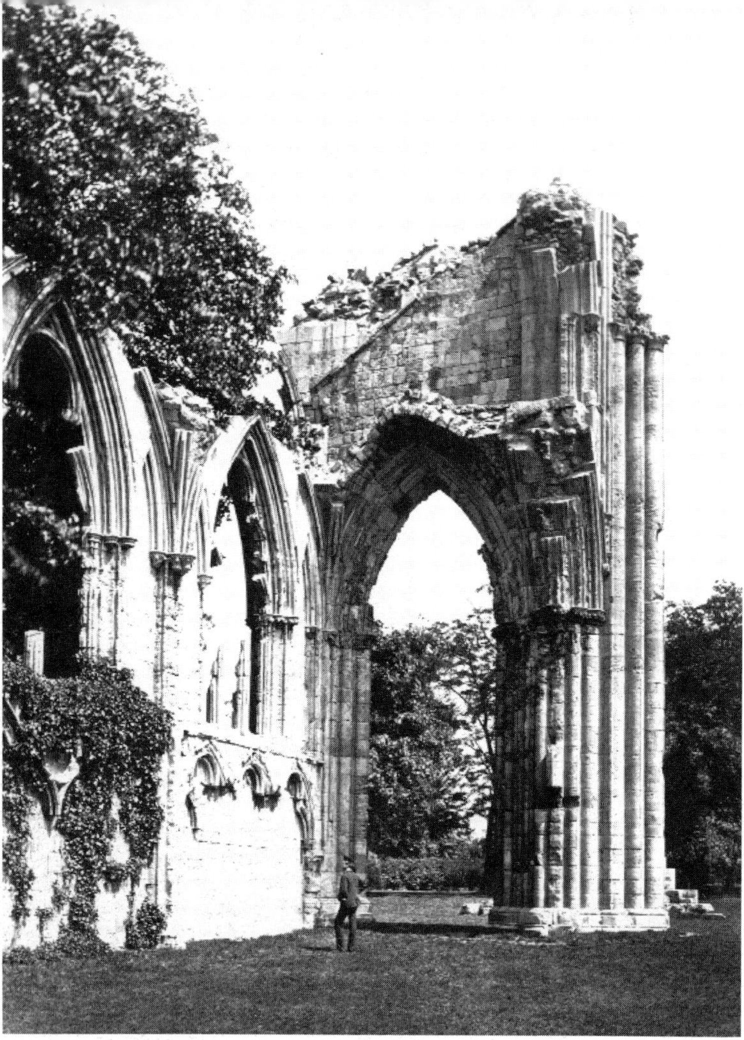

ST MARY'S ABBEY
c1873 / 6619

The south face was undergoing repair work at this time. Pollution, mainly from the smoke from the railways, did a lot of damage to both glass and stone. Between 1829 to 1984, there were three fires; the first was caused deliberately, the second was caused by a careless workman, and the third by lightning. All three caused terrible damage and loss, but we may be thankful that major restoration work was carried out.

THE MINSTER

c1890 / Y12501

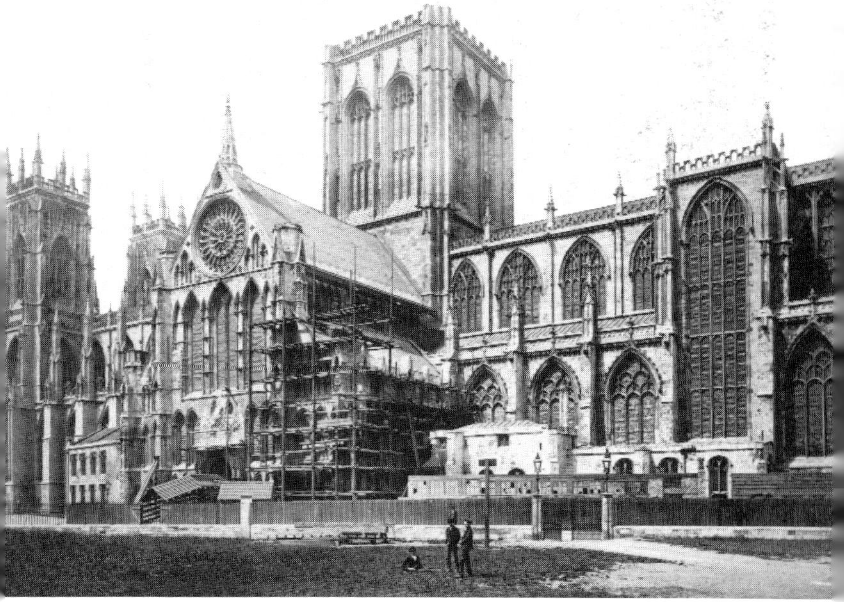

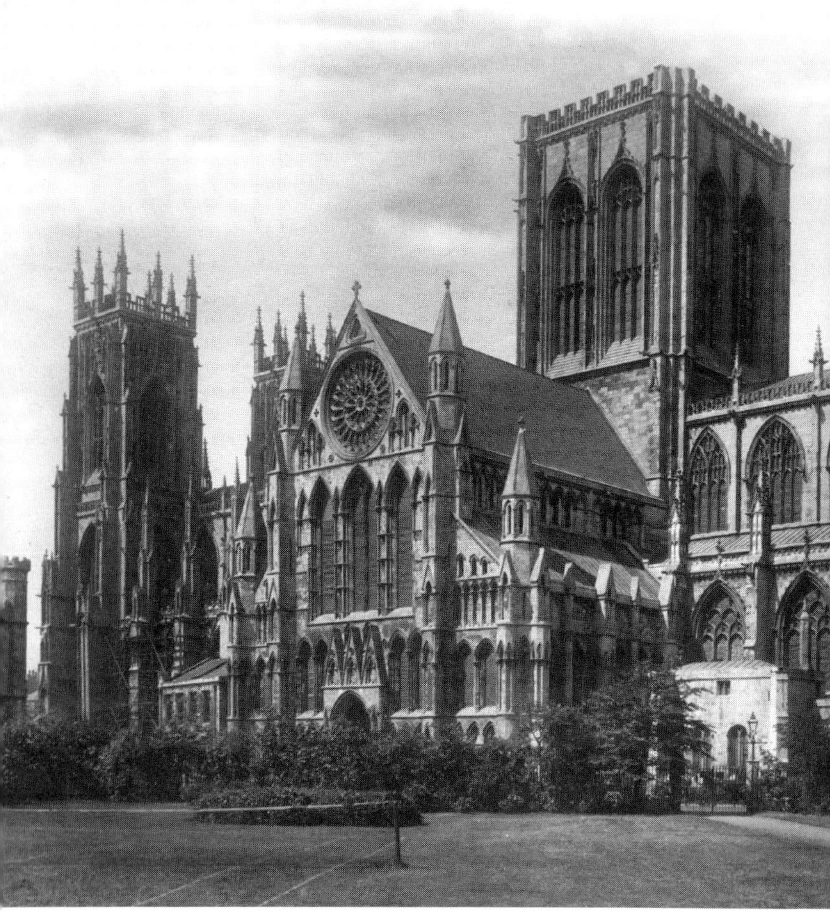

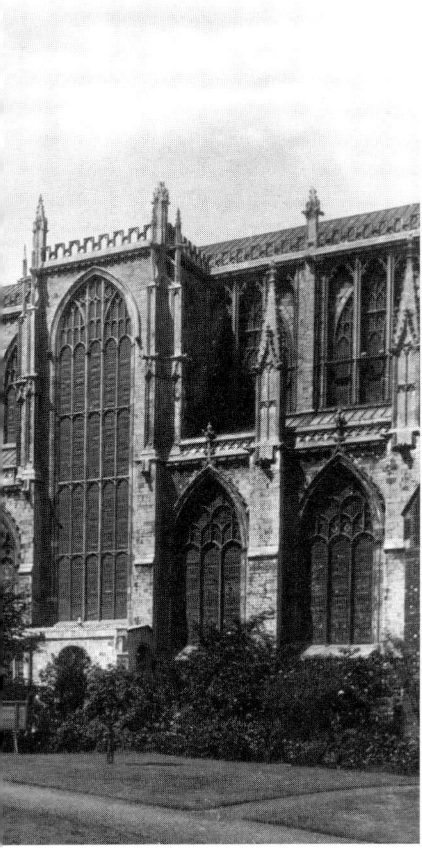

There has been very little change to the appearance of this magnificent structure owing to careful restoration and repair, but the surroundings of the Minster have altered. On the grass to the left a statue of Constantine the Great, the Roman Emperor in 306, has been erected, and the roads are now much closer and almost surround the building.

THE MINSTER

1897 / 39491

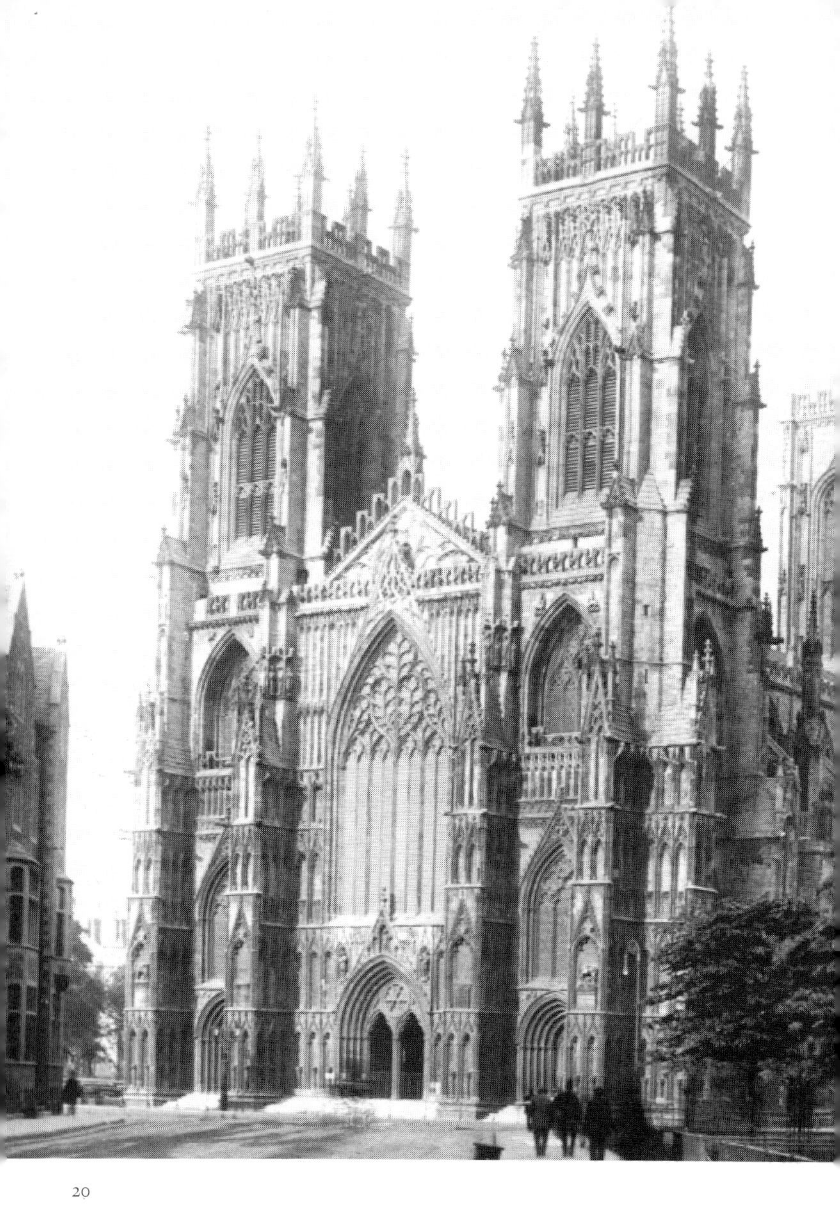

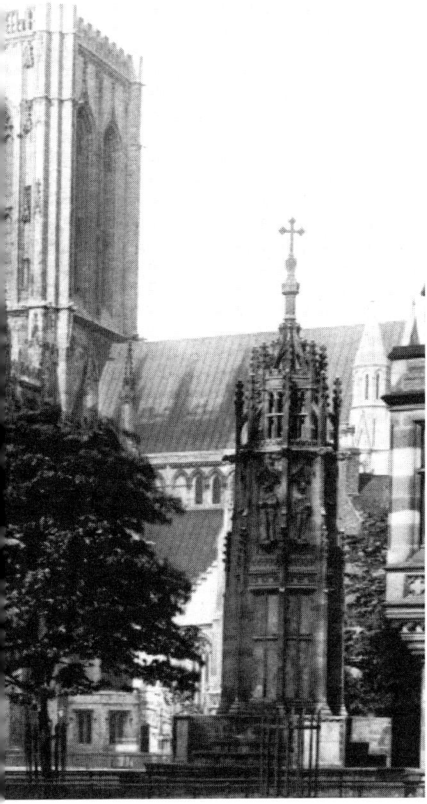

To the right of this view is Duncombe Place, with the tall memorial to the soldiers who took part in the Boer War. It was erected in 1905. One of the six statues that encircled it is now missing because lightning struck the memorial. The cross that crowned the memorial has also gone.

THE MINSTER
1908 / 59785

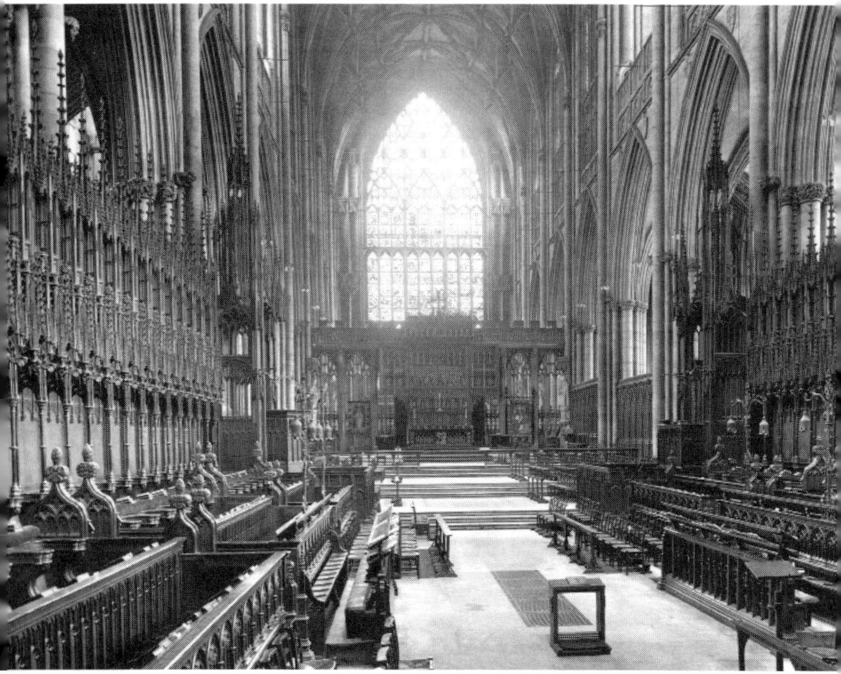

Here we can see the huge size of the magnificent stained glass window above the high altar. Made in the 13th century, it is larger than a tennis court. Releading of the window was begun when it was removed during the second world war for safety; the mammoth task took ten years to complete.

THE MINSTER

CHOIR EAST *1921* / 70640

This, the northern gate, stands on the site of the Roman Porta Principalis, the gateway of Eboracum. The barbican was demolished in 1835. The name Bootham derives from Buthum, 'at the booths'; this probably related to market stalls that were set up nearby. The medieval statues that can just be seen on the top of the bar are in very poor condition and are hardly recognisable as figures.

BOOTHAM BAR

1886 / 18443

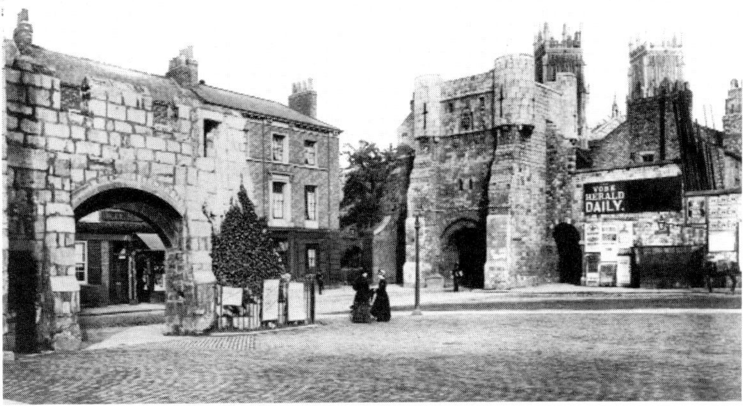

This was the gateway that led to the road to London. In the 10th century, when permission was granted for a house to be built on the bar, the yearly rent charged was sixpence. Eventually Micklegate commanded the highest rent of the four bars: just over 13s. The walls of the passage are built with Roman stone, including used coffins.

The heads of traitors and conspirators were often displayed on pikes here up until 1754, when the government called a halt to this practice because two of the heads were stolen by a Jacobite tailor. He was caught and fined £5 and sentenced to two years in jail. There are stories of ghosts frequenting the bar, including a gentleman dressed in black.

MICKLEGATE BAR

1886 / 18439

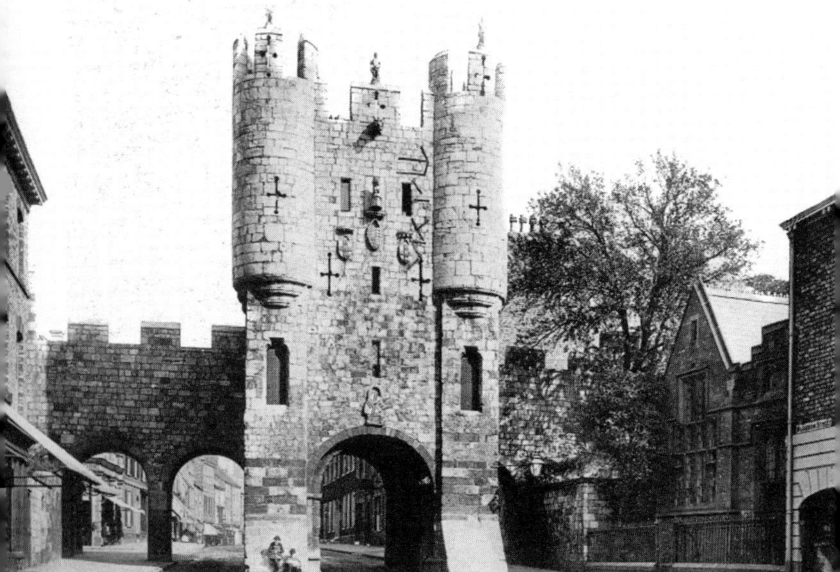

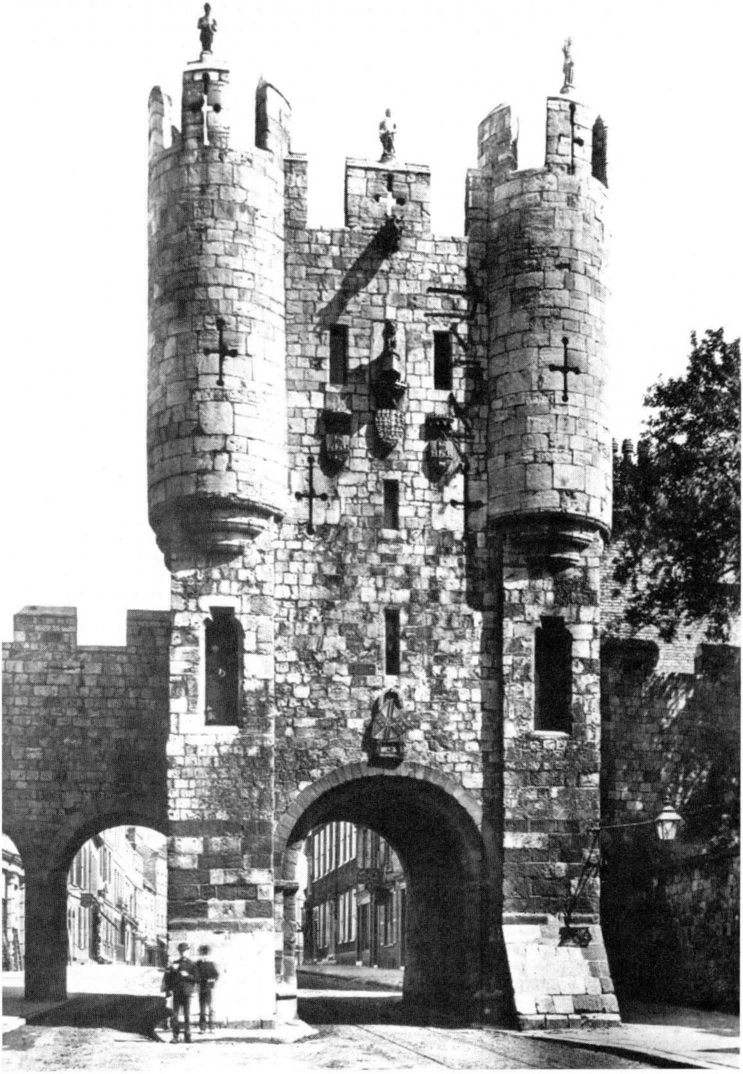

MICKLEGATE BAR

c1885 / 18440

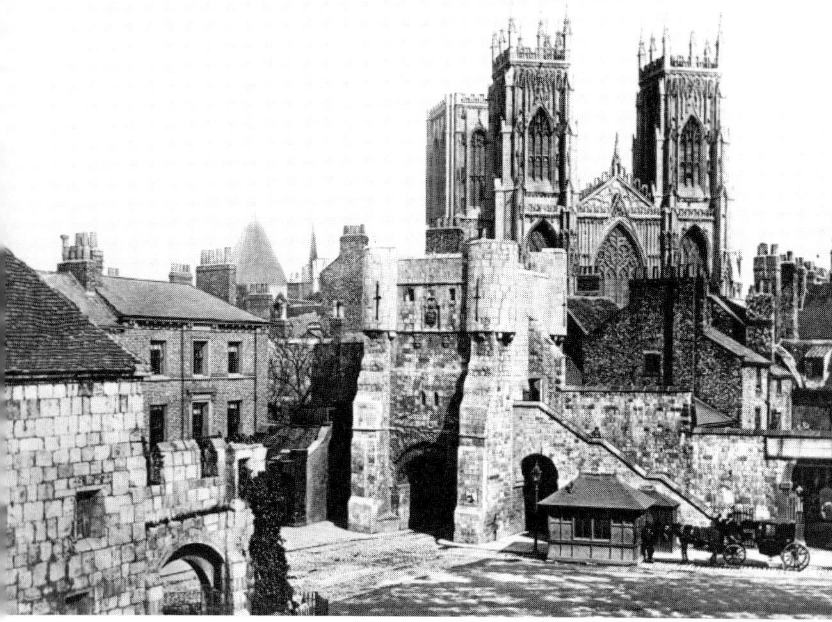

The stone-arched building on the right was the postern tower built in 1497 on St Mary's Abbey walls; it is now an office for First York Buses. The little cabmen's shelter at the side of the bar is no longer there. To the rear right of the bar we can see the turret on the roof of the Minster Chapter House.

BOOTHAM BAR AND THE MINSTER

1893 / 32032

The archway to this bar dates from the 11th century; this is the oldest of York's gates. In medieval times, guards were posted to keep watch and to guide people from the nearby Forest of Galtres so as to protect them from the packs of wolves that roamed the area.

BOOTHAM BAR

1909 / 61701

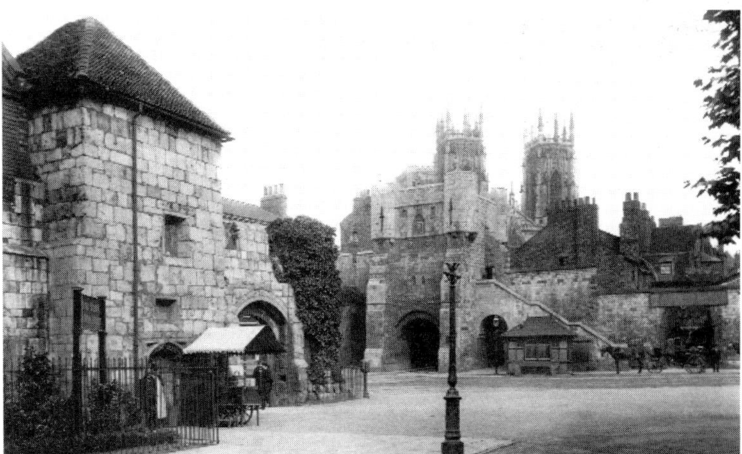

Carved in 1894 by George Milburn, the statues on the top of the bar replaced the older, worn statues. The figures that now look down are Nicholas Langton, a Lord Mayor, a mason holding a model of the bar and a medieval knight. The coats of arms are the Stuart Royal Arms and the City Arms; these were renewed in 1969.

BOOTHAM BAR

1911 / 63585

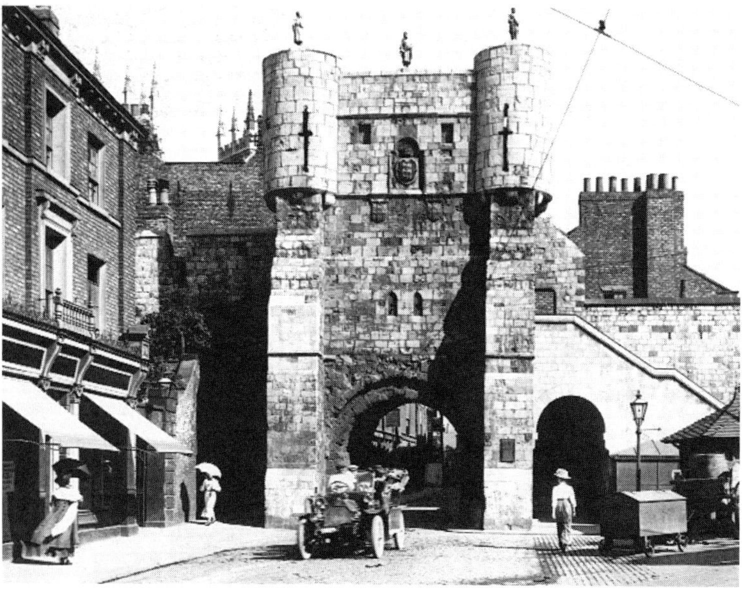

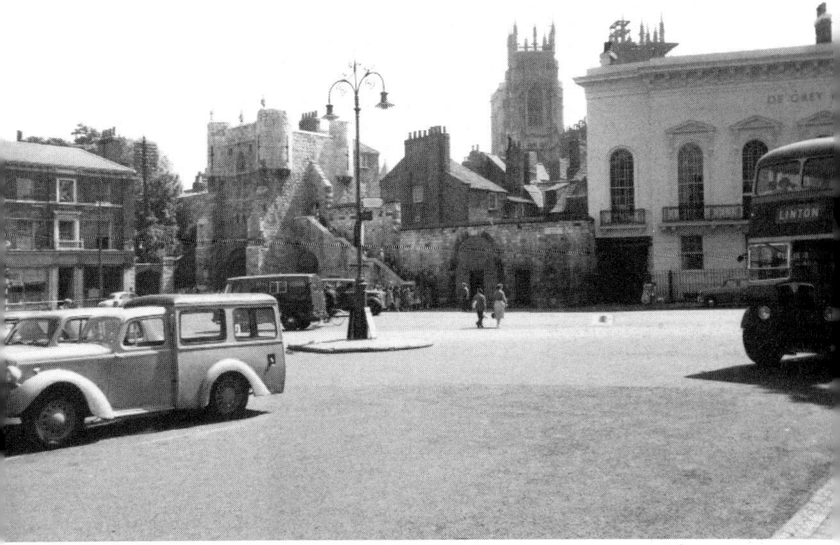

This view is taken from St Leonard's Place. The De Grey Rooms to the right were built in about 1841. The building was once used by the Yorkshire Hussars as an officers' mess; it is now the York Tourist Information Centre. The bus is heading for Linton-on-Ouse.

BOOTHAM BAR

C1955 / Y12031

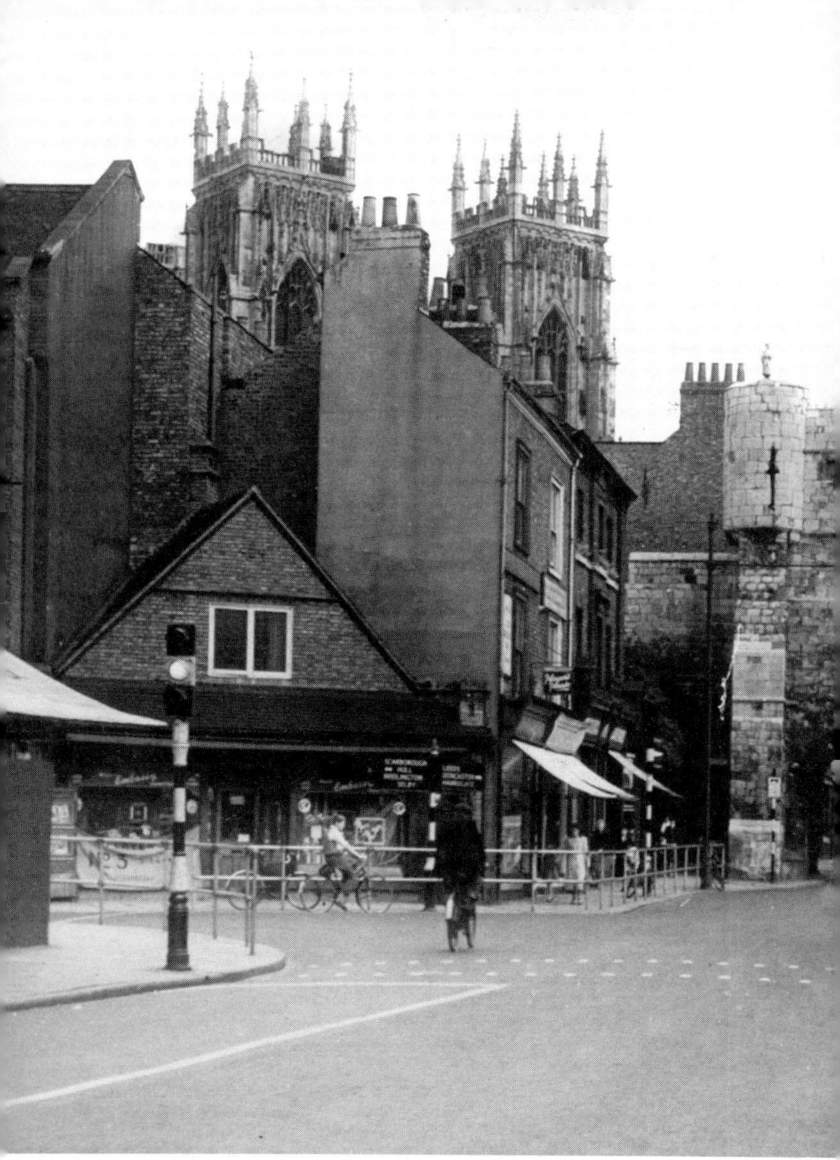

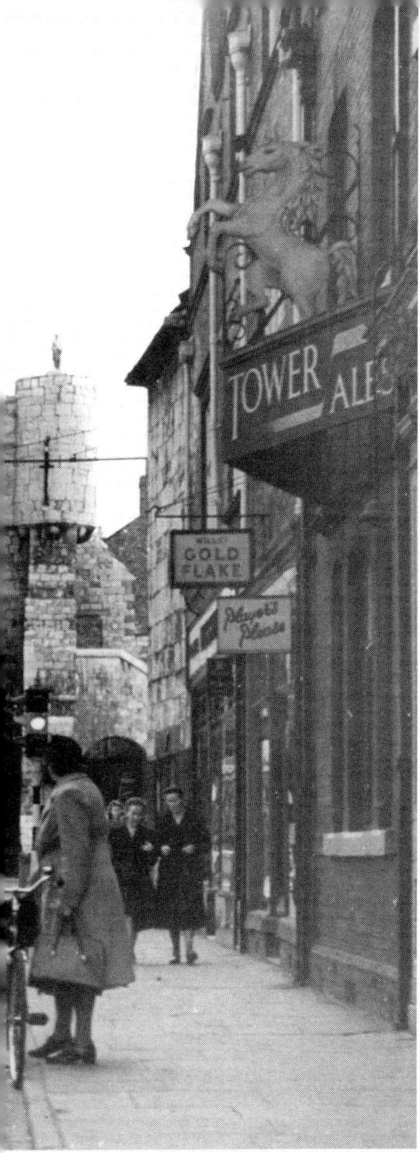

The public house on the right is The White Horse; the statue of a horse can be seen rearing above the Tower Ales sign. Towards the bar old stonework still remains, with a sign for Pullman's Coaches. To the left, the corner shop with the large awning is now a bookmakers. These once quiet roads are now filled with heavy traffic.

BOOTHAM BAR

c1950 / Y12008

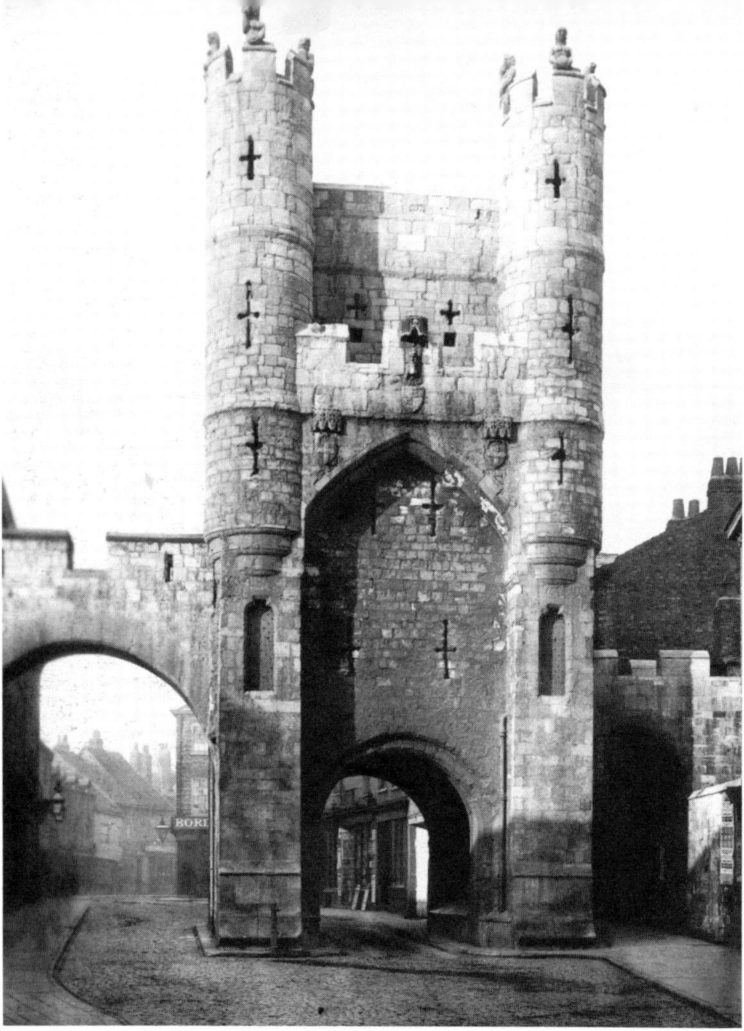

MONK BAR
c1885 / 18442

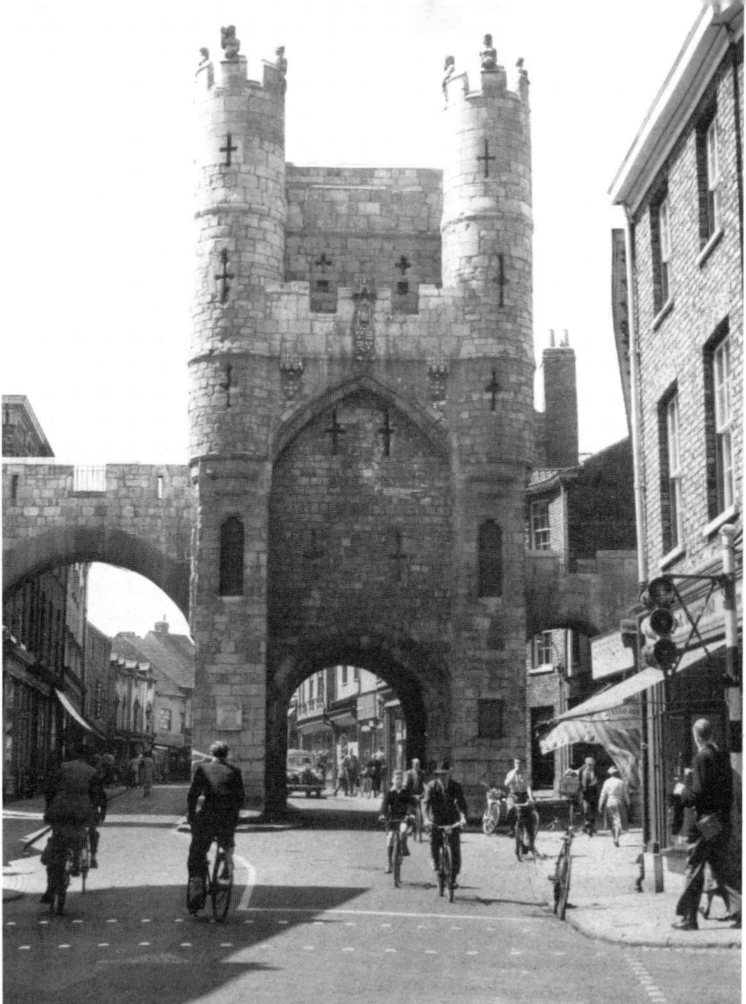

MONK BAR
c1950 / Y12019

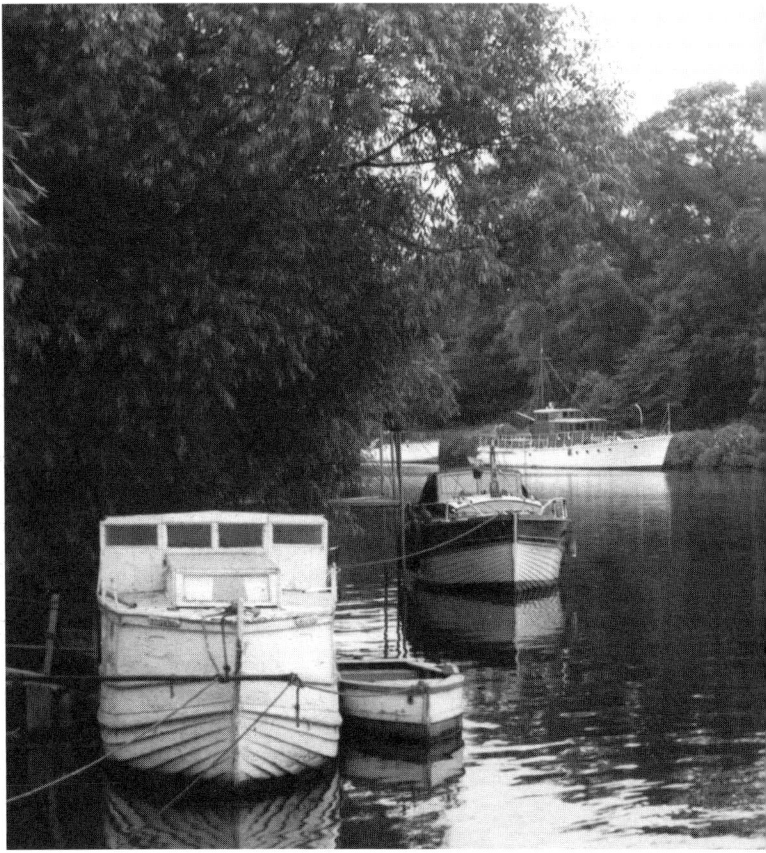

NABURN

THE RIVER c1955 / N72012

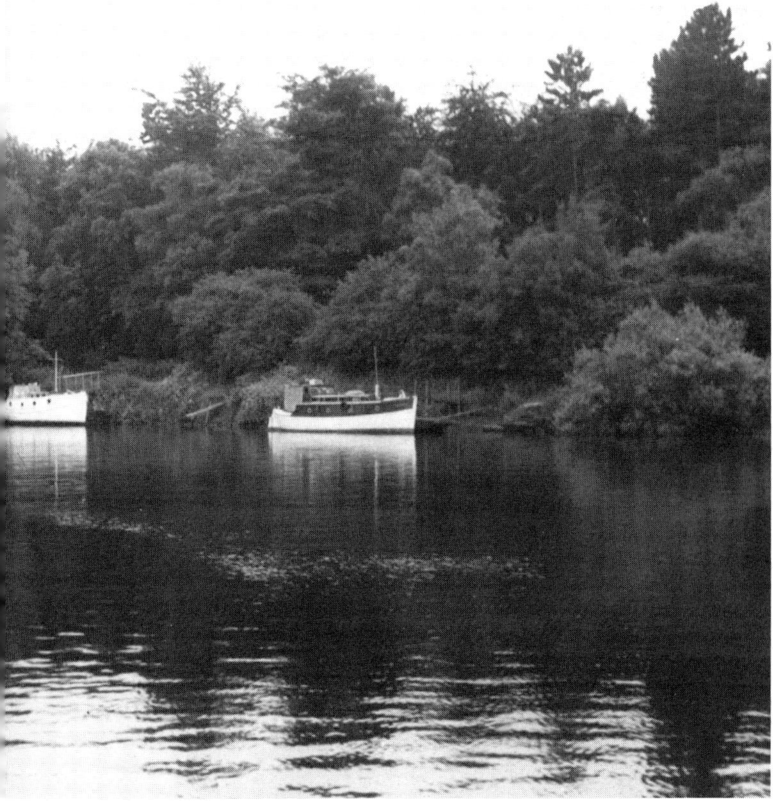

Naburn is situated four miles south of York. In 1757 a weir and a lock were built to accommodate the river traffic. Once the water could hardly be seen for the many barges packing the river from bank to bank, carrying their vast variety of cargo from Hull to York.

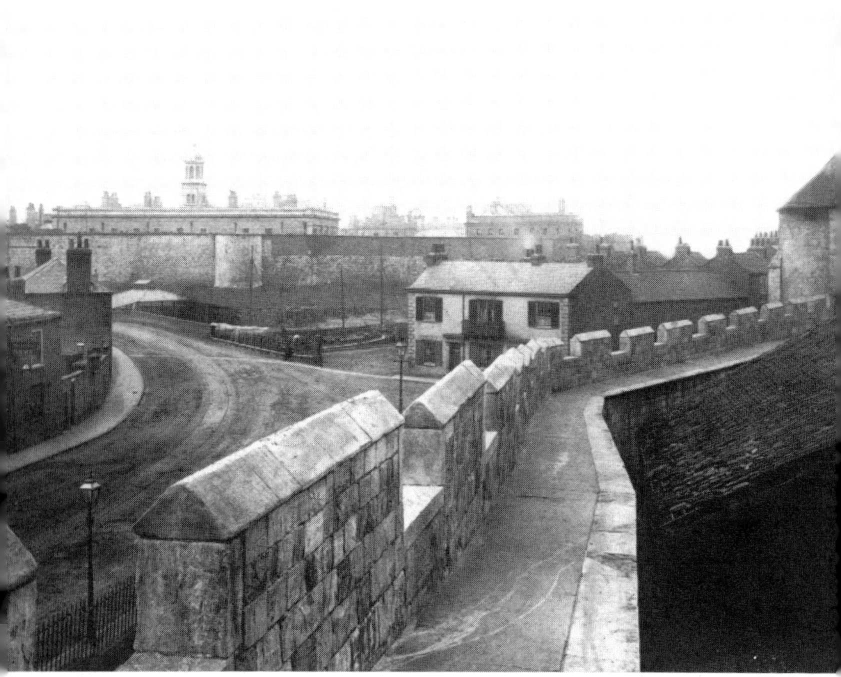

The forbidding walls that surround the castle can be seen in the background. Originally there were six postern towers; the one at Fishergate is now the only one that remains unaltered. It once overlooked the King's Fishpool. On the first floor there was a lavatory that projected out over the lake.

YORK CASTLE

FISHERGATE POSTERN c1885 / 18496

We are looking towards Ouse Bridge with South Esplanade on the right. The view has remained virtually the same, except for the difference in the river traffic and a change of use for some of the buildings. There are still private houses here, while others are now restaurants and bed and breakfasts catering for the many visitors.

VIEW FROM SKELDERGATE BRIDGE

c1885 / 18464

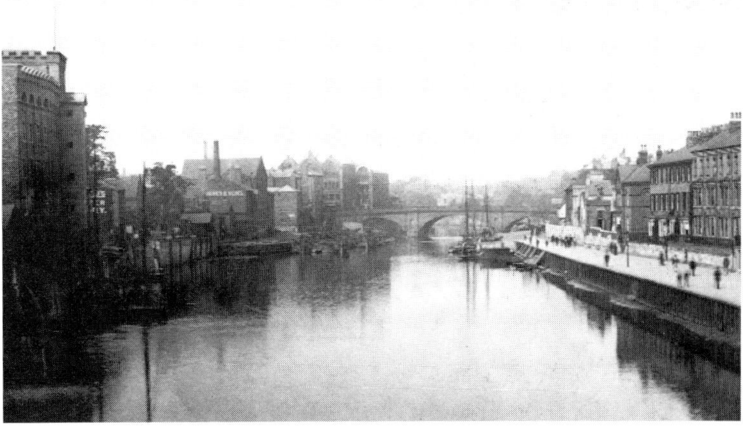

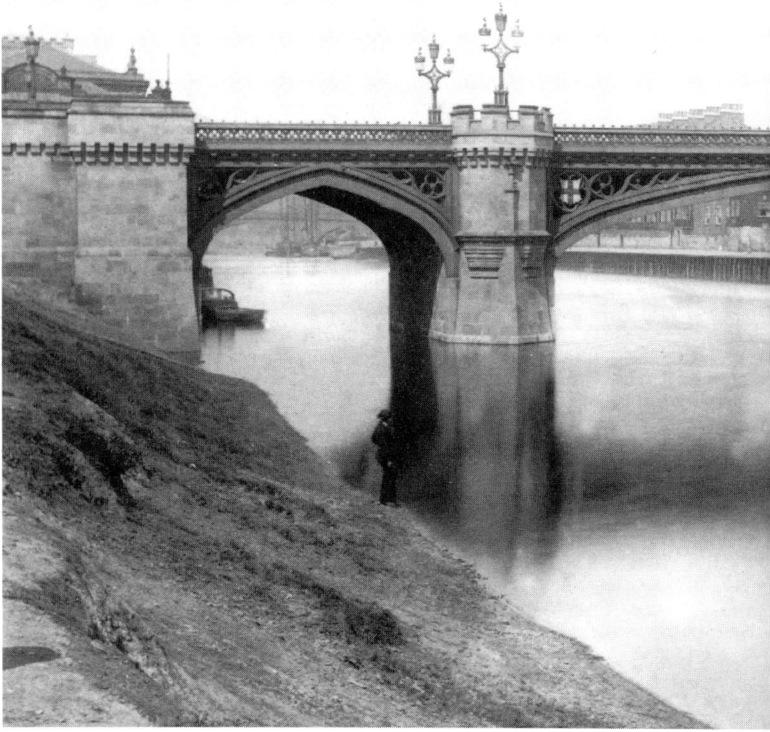

SKELDERGATE BRIDGE
c1885 / 18457

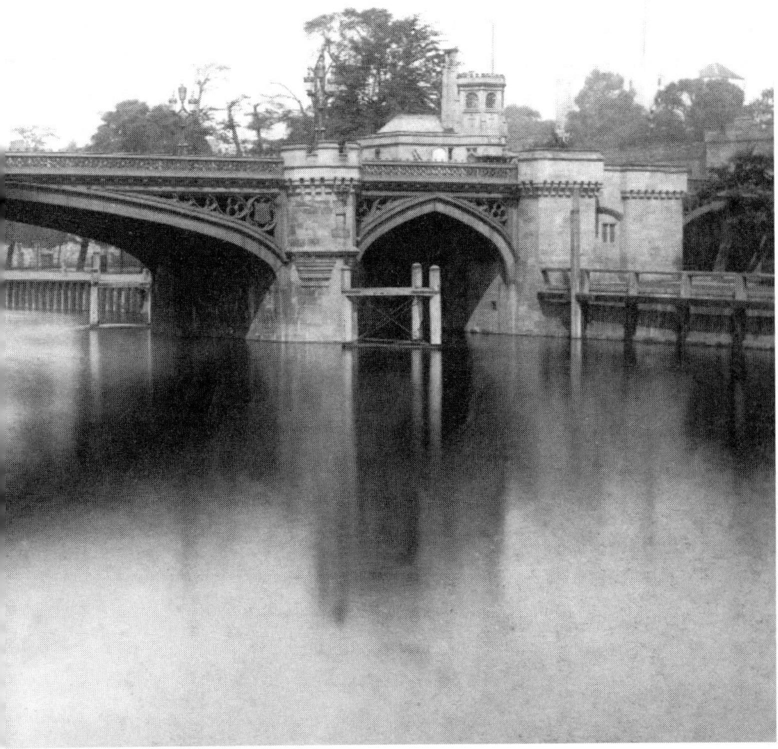

The little castle-like building on the right of the bridge still remains. It was the toll house, and until 1914 it cost a halfpenny to cross. Opposite, in St George's Field, was the ducking stool used for scoundrels and females who served false measures or brewed bad beer.

Built in the 12th century, the original bridge was of wood and was probably sited nearer the Guildhall. Shops and houses, perhaps as many as fifty, were built on it. In 1565 the bridge collapsed. The new structure was rebuilt in stone later in the 16th century. The present bridge was built in the early 19th century.

OUSE BRIDGE
1885 / 18463

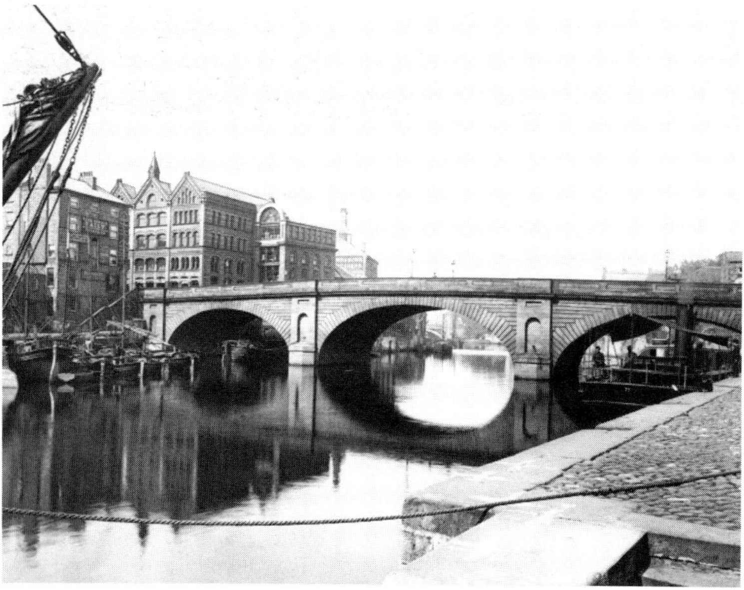

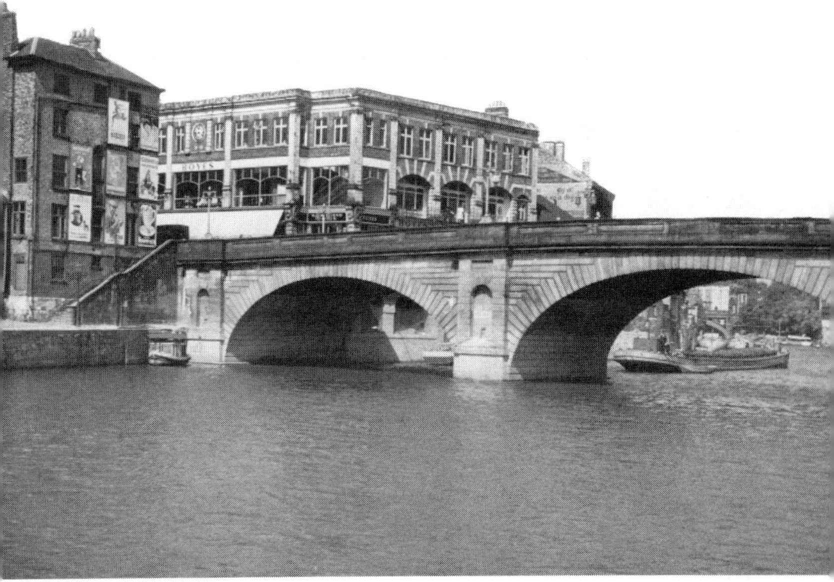

The story is told (which may or may not be true) that in 1154 thousands of people lined the old bridge to herald the arrival of Archbishop William Fitzherbert, later to become St William of York. The weight of the crowds caused the bridge to collapse, but no-one was killed; because there was no loss of life, it was proclaimed a miracle.

OUSE BRIDGE
c1950 / Y12005

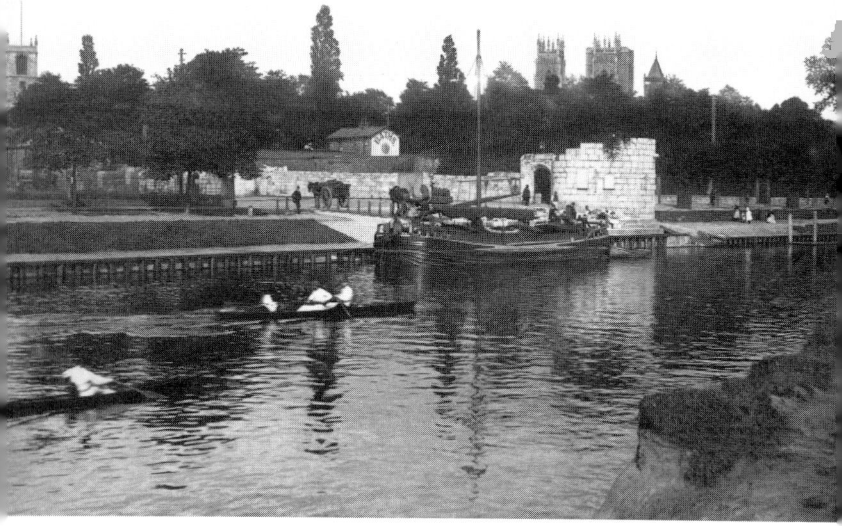

This was the water tower for St Mary's Abbey. At one time the abbey boundary wall stood along the river bank. The little building to the rear, which here has 'baths' written on it, is now used as a store for canoes. The cart horses and their owners are waiting patiently to unload cargo from the moored boat - was it fish, perhaps?

ST MARY'S TOWER

c1885 / 18455

This tower was once linked by a chain to Barker's Tower on the opposite side of the river to stop craft entering the city without paying a tax. From the 17th century it was a pumping house for the town's water supply - the wheel was turned by horses. Nearby we can see the York Water Works Offices.

LENDAL TOWER

C1885 / 18456

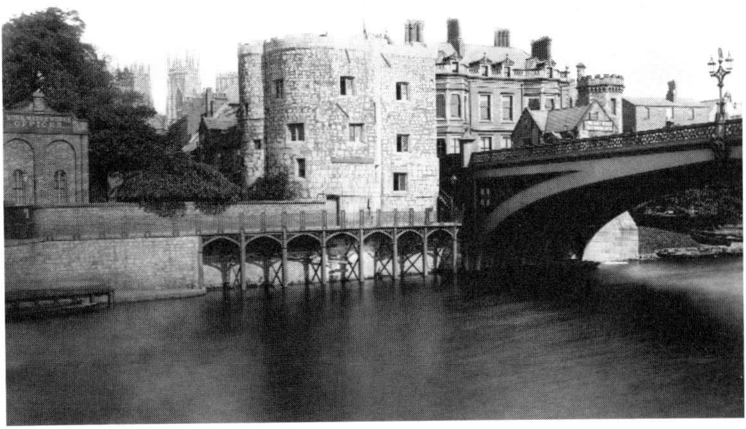

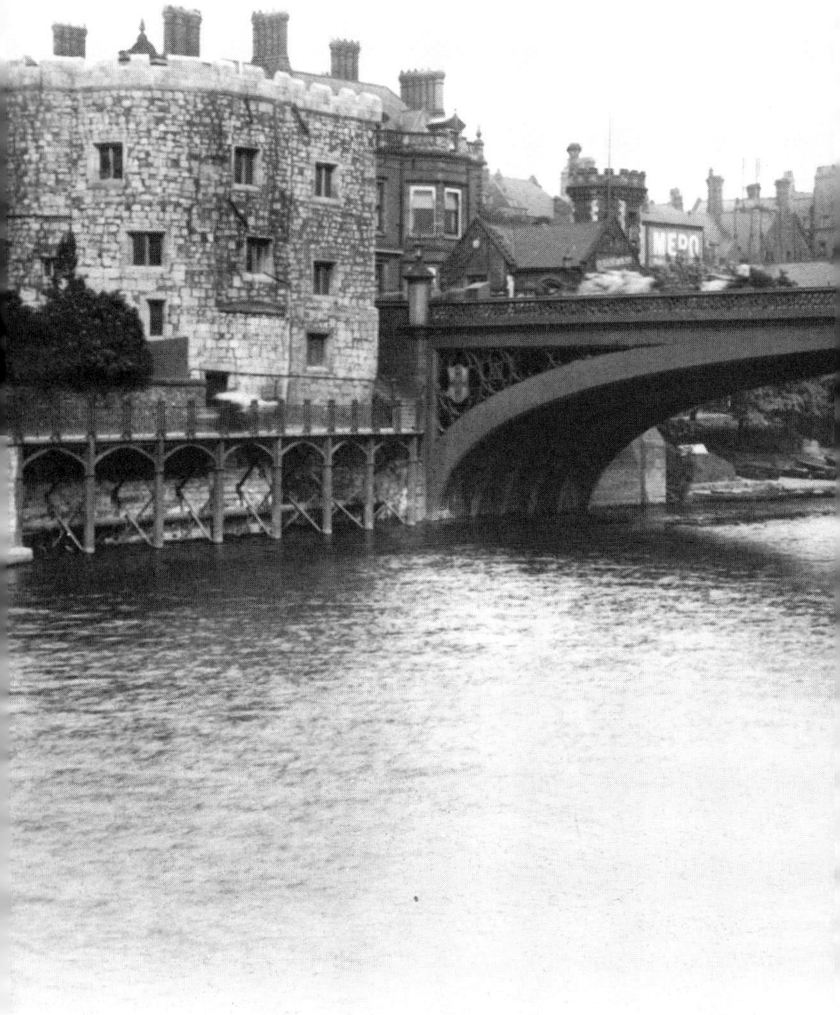
MERO

LENDAL BRIDGE

1909 / 61702

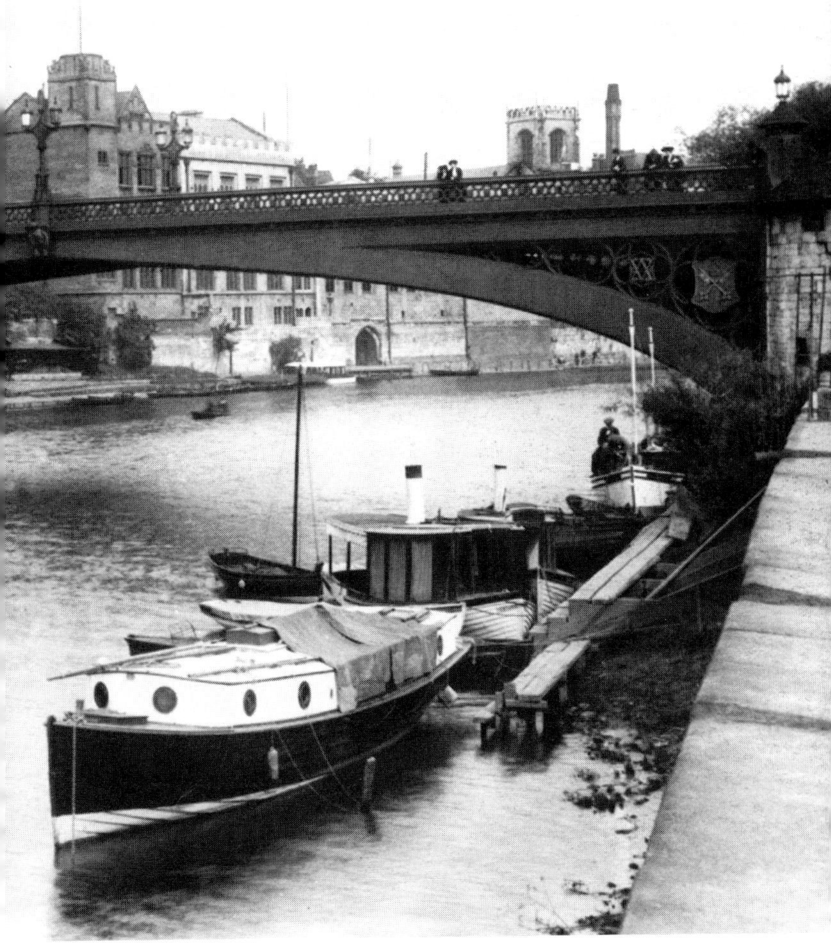

In this later view, we can see the Guildhall on the left side of the riverbank. As well as an underground passage opening right onto the water's edge, the Guildhall has two secret rooms. By the time of this photograph, the river was being used more and more for pleasure: streamlined boats are moored by the bank, and a canoe with its lone occupant is heading towards Lendal Bridge.

THE RIVER

C1950 / Y12021

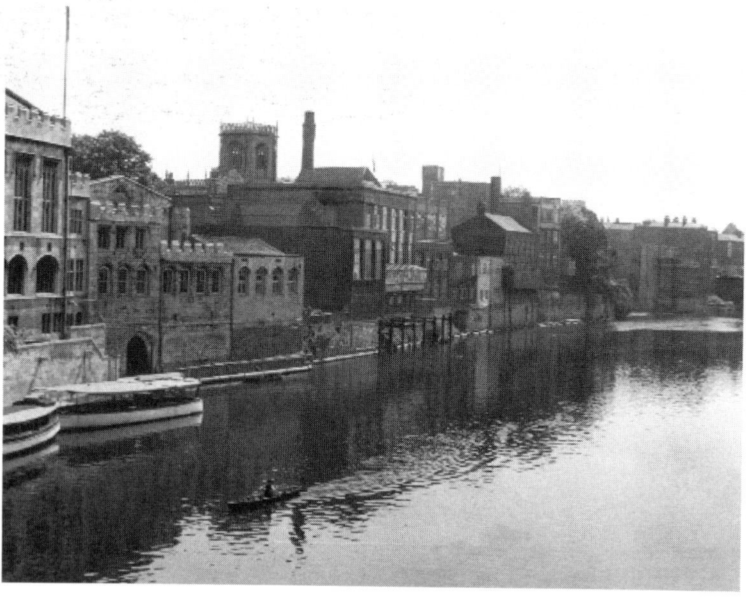

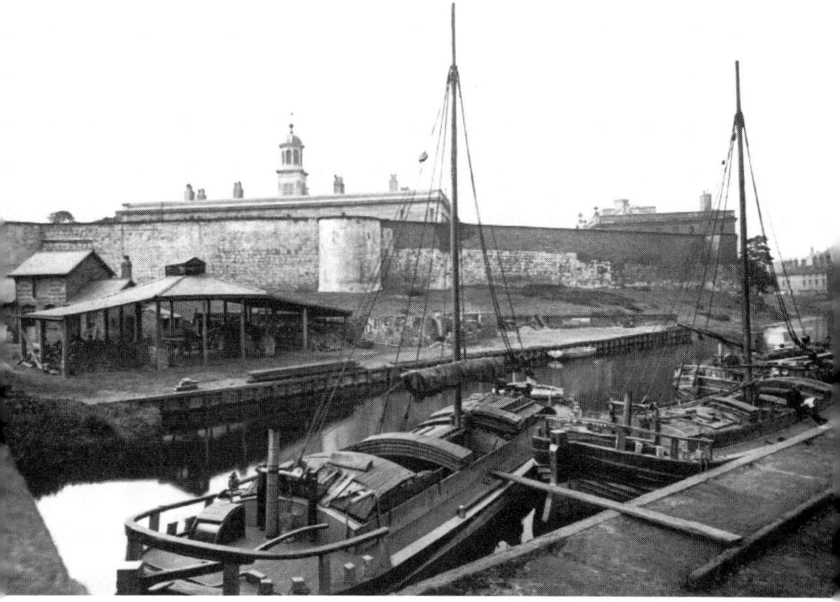

The first recorded wooden bridge was built in 1583, and was destroyed during the siege of York. Two more were built after one another; the second was washed away by floods. This photograph, showing the castle walls and the dome of the Debtors' Prison, was taken from the fourth recorded bridge, which was replaced by the present one in 1955 owing to the demands of traffic.

THE CASTLE
FROM CASTLE MILL BRIDGE

1885 / 18494

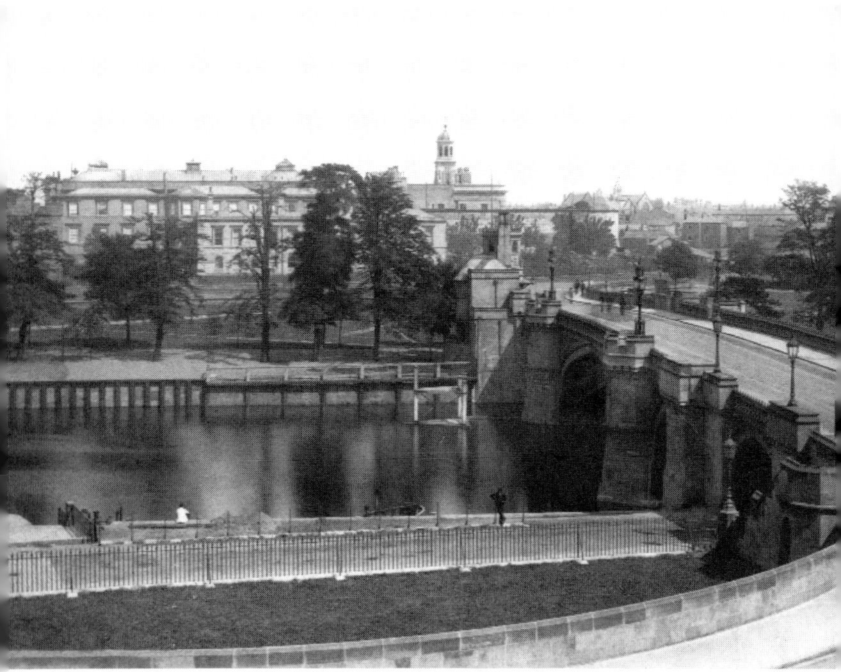

This wonderful view from the walls was taken before the onslaught of the motor car, and when gas lamps were still in place. As we look east over Skeldergate Bridge and the River Ouse to the left we can see the Assize Court; to the centre, standing out against the skyline is the spire of what was the Debtors' Prison and is now the Castle Museum.

YORK CASTLE
C1885 / 18489

This panoramic view takes in Lendal Tower, the Assize Court and the towers of the Minster in the distance. Outside the walls along the section near the hotel and station was a burial ground. Many of the victims of the cholera epidemic of 1832 were laid to rest there.

VIEW FROM THE STATION HOTEL

c1885 / 18432

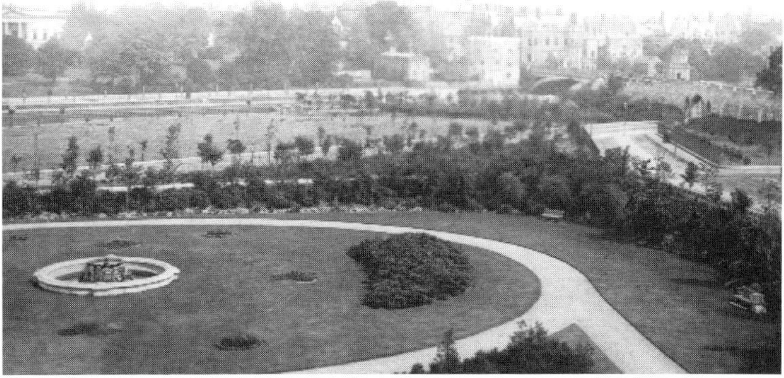

This and the following three photos, although from the same vantage point, span a period of 60 years. They show many changes in some of the buildings and in the mode of transport. Two horse-drawn vehicles can be seen on the road, and some people in their finery, the ladies twirling parasols, are on foot. Perhaps it is a Sunday and they are heading for church.

VIEW FROM THE CITY WALLS

1897 / 39492

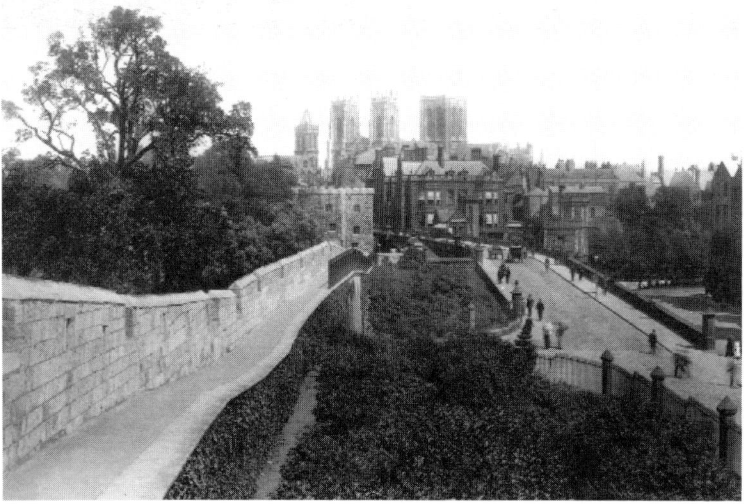

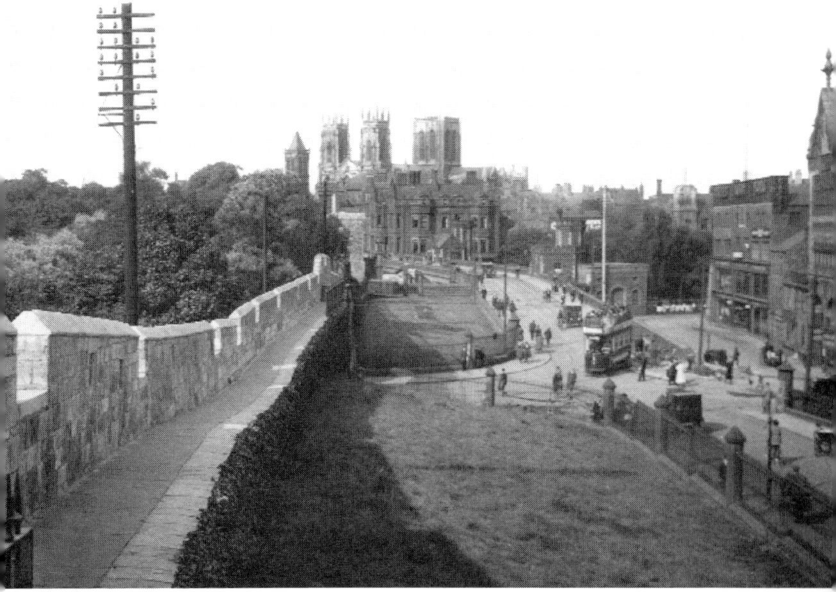

To the right of the view, the tall building, built in 1884, was Walker's Repository for Horses; later, the building was shortened to about half its height. A lone tram trundles around the corner, and a few cars can be seen. To the rear of the photograph, on the right of the Minster, stands the smaller tower of St Wilfred's Church, which was built in 1864 and still stands.

THE MINSTER FROM THE CITY WALLS

1921 / 70637

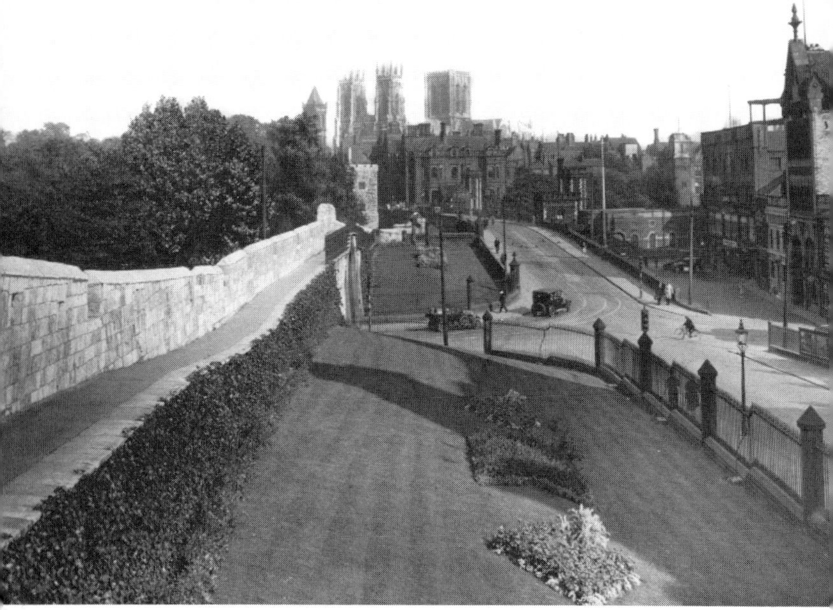

It is nearly 20 years later, and the area to the right is now completely built up. On the left, where the road sweeps round the corner, is the toll house for Lendal Bridge, built in 1863; it is now used as a teashop. The tram lines are plainly visible. Cars were still an unaffordable item to many, as we can see here from the almost empty roads.

THE MINSTER
FROM THE CITY WALLS
C1940 / Y12010

There have been many more changes to the buildings on the right, and now the tram lines have been removed; road markings, showing a one-way system, have taken their place. Cars and a bus form a queue heading for the city centre. The flower bed depicts the logo for the York Festival.

THE MINSTER FROM THE CITY WALLS

C1955 / Y12074

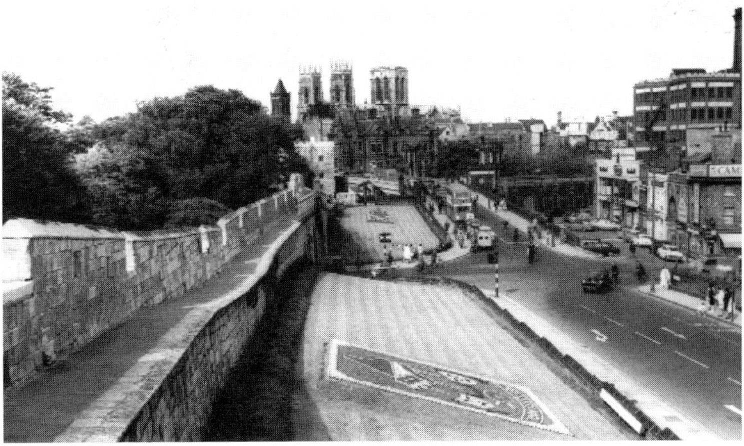

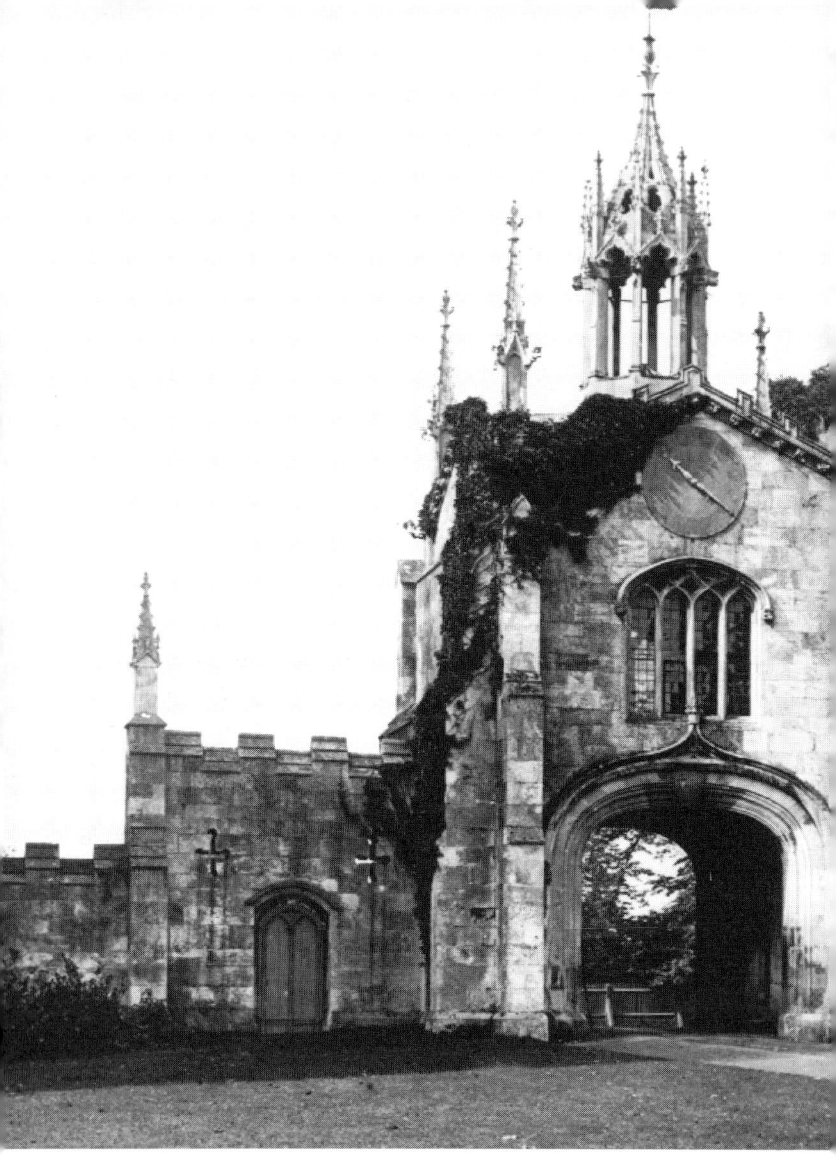

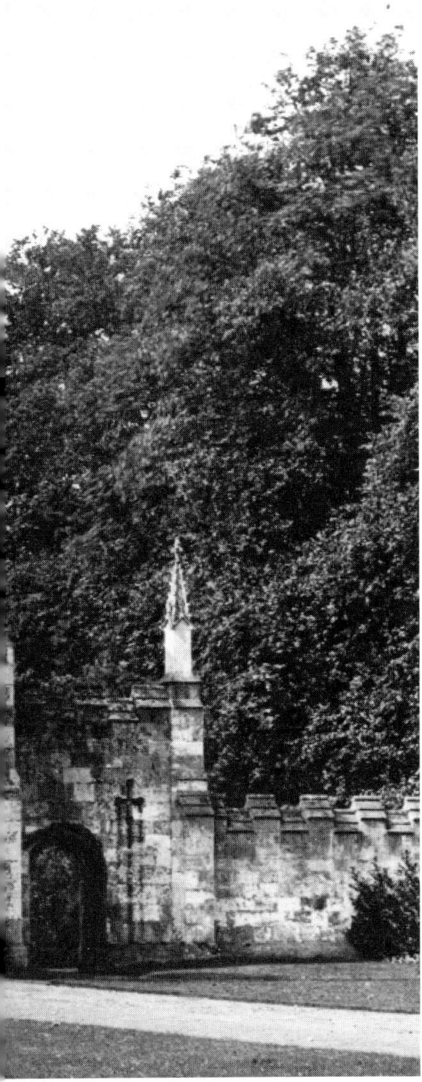

The palace was built by the 33rd Archbishop of York, Walter de Gray, in about 1250, using stone from a previous manor house that he had had demolished. There is a large amount of wonderful medieval stained glass in the building, including the shields of nineteen of the past archbishops in the dining room.

BISHOPTHORPE
PALACE GATE
c1885 / 18499

Extensions were added to the palace over the following century after it was first built. Then in 1647 Bishopthorpe was sold to a Colonel White, who added further to the building. During the Restoration the palace reverted to the church, and the great hall was rebuilt. Later, stables and another extension on the west side were added.

BISHOPTHORPE PALACE FROM THE DRIVE

1893 / 32045

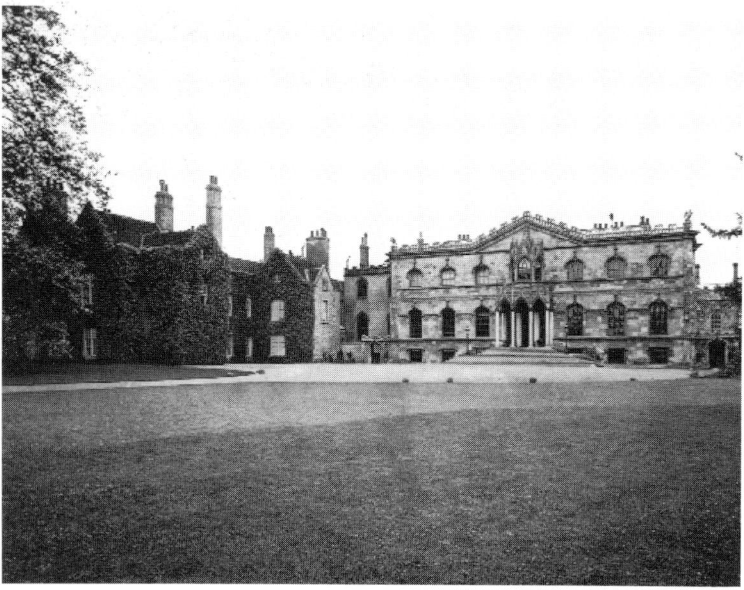

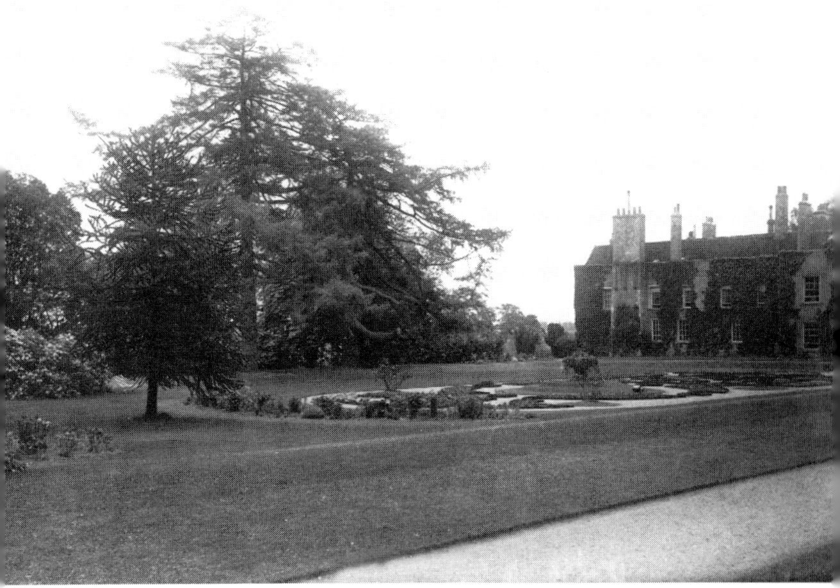

Originally the village was known as Thorpe St Andrew; the name was changed to Bishopthorpe because of the archbishop's palace being built here. One can imagine the bishops using these peaceful gardens for prayer and meditation.

BISHOPTHORPE PALACE GARDENS

1893 / 32047

BISHOPTHORPE PALACE FROM THE RIVER

1893 / 32044

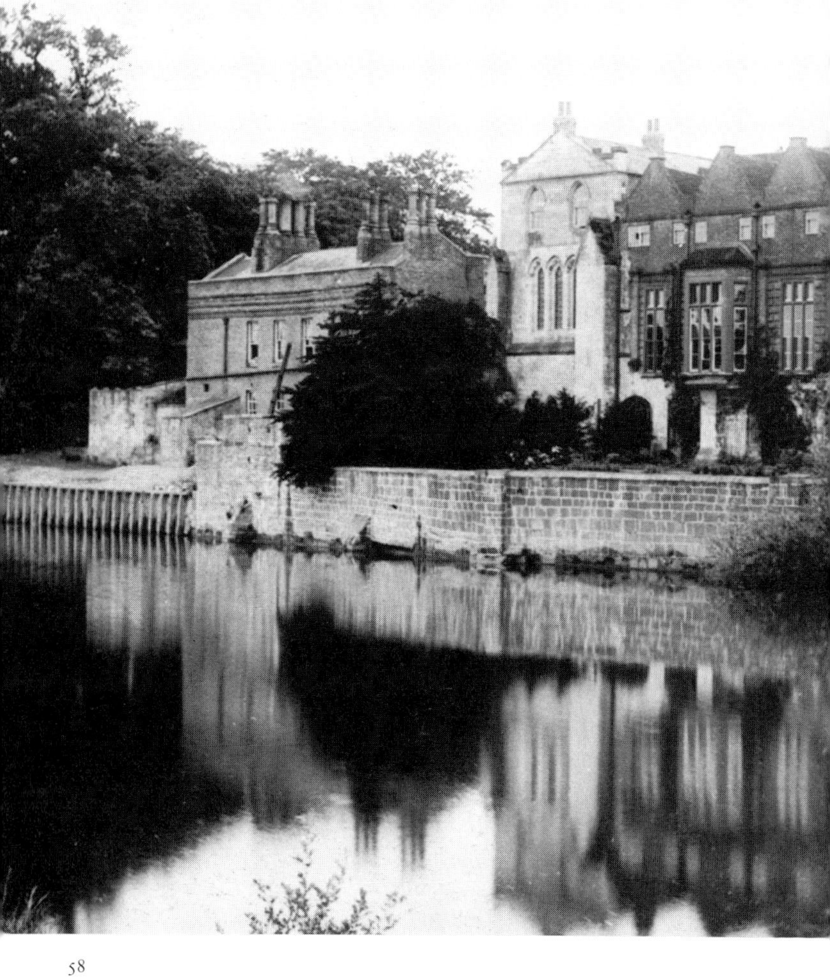

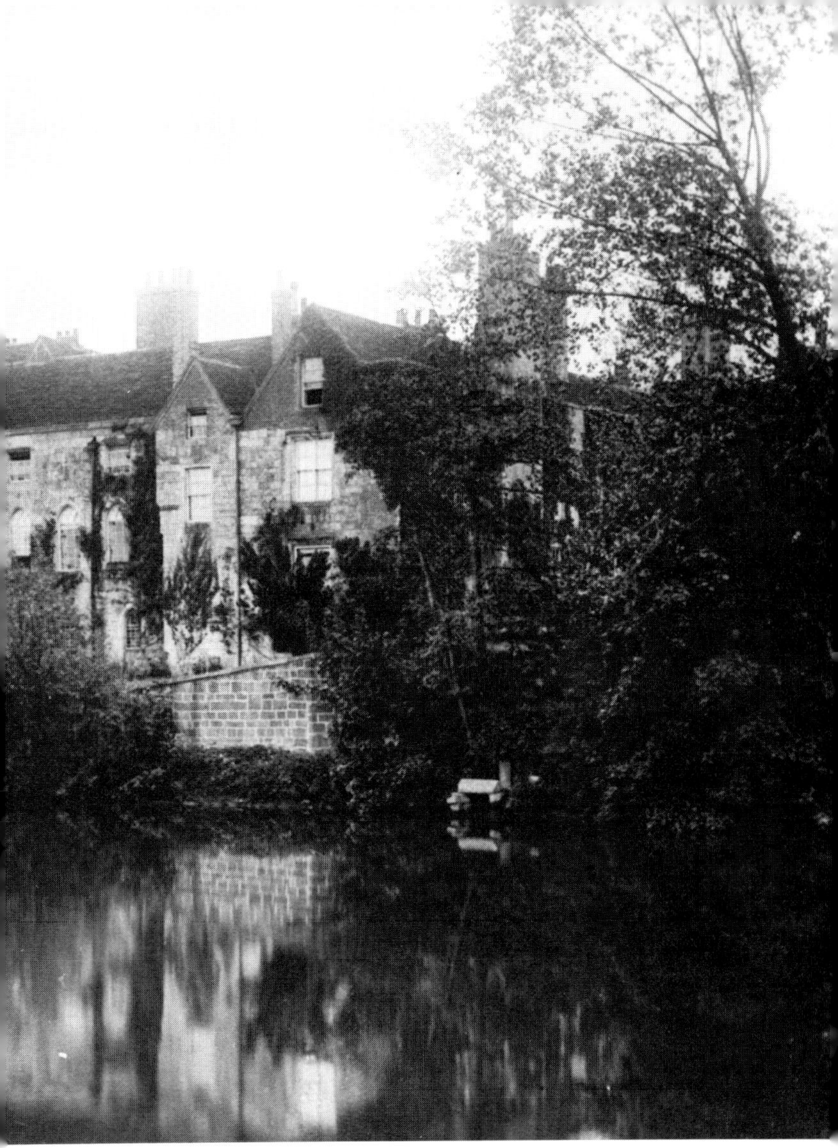

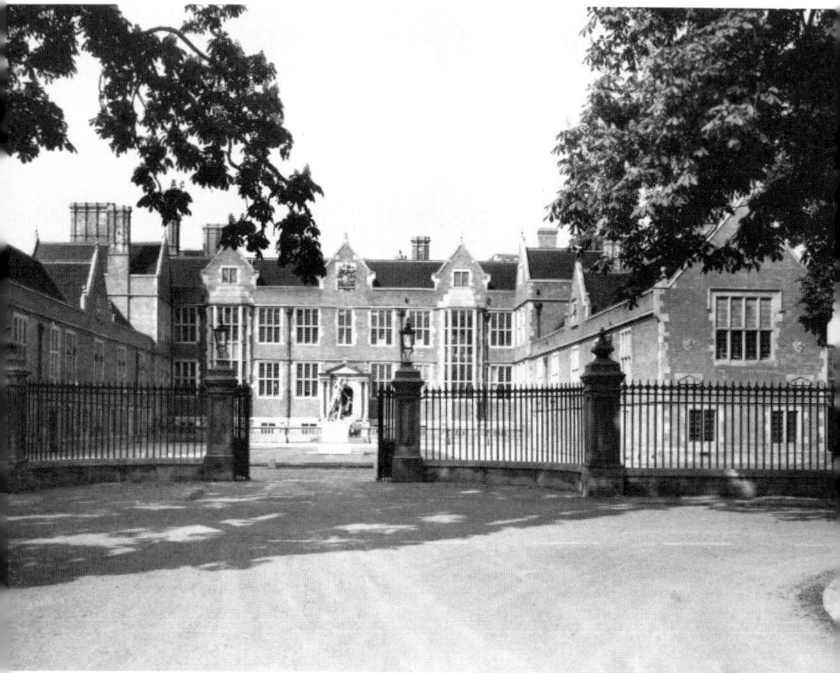

This elegant Elizabethan mansion was originally built for the Secretary of the Council of the North in 1568. The hall changed hands many times over the following centuries before being almost rebuilt in the mid 19th century. The university became established here in 1963; it now has a total of more than 3,000 students.

HESLINGTON HALL

THE UNIVERSITY OF YORK C1960 / Y12082

This, the main body of the university, is spread over approximately 190 acres. The university uses many of the historical buildings in the city, as well as the Hall. The statue, the Goddess Diana, was removed after being damaged during student unrest in the 1970s.

HESLINGTON HALL

THE UNIVERSITY OF YORK c1960 / Y12080

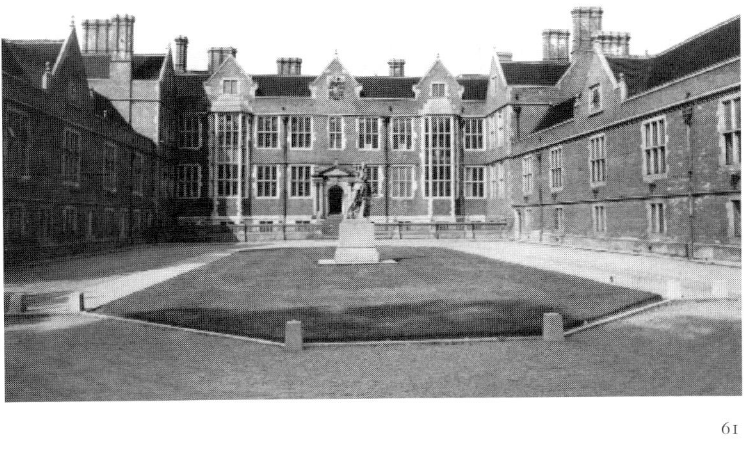

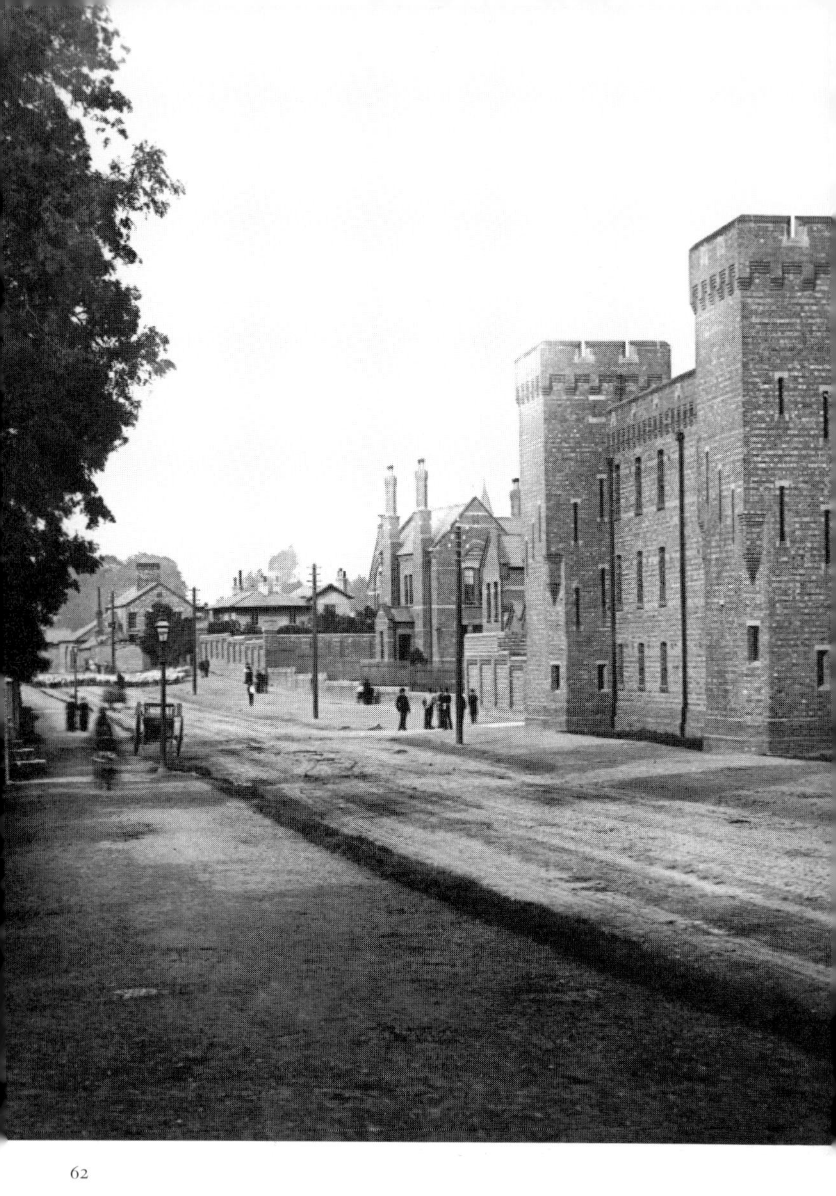

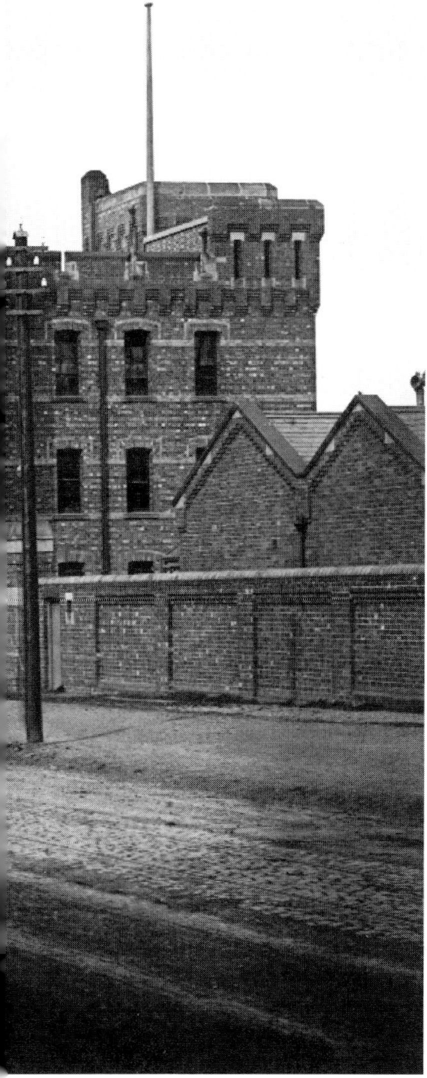

York was a military centre, and over 1,000 men were stationed here when the barracks were built. They had their own hospital and a soldiers' institute. Tower Street housed the armoury for the West Yorkshire Volunteer Artillery, and the York Volunteer Rifles were in St Andrewgate. The soldiers' superior officer has let them stand at ease for the camera!

THE INFANTRY BARRACKS

THE ARMOURY 1886 / 18705

Situated on Fulford Road, the barracks were originally built around 1795 for the 14th Regimental District and the West Yorkshire Regiment. In 1951, to commemorate exploits in India, the site became known as the Imphal Barracks. The large keep on view here is still in use. A 25-pounder gun and a Saladin armoured car are preserved on the site.

THE INFANTRY BARRACKS

THE ARMOURY 1886 / 18710

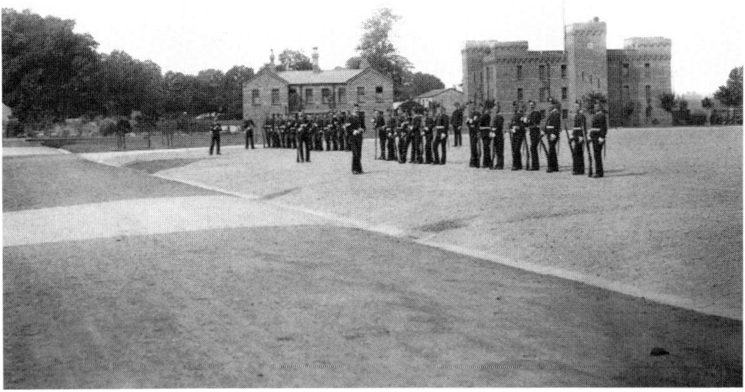

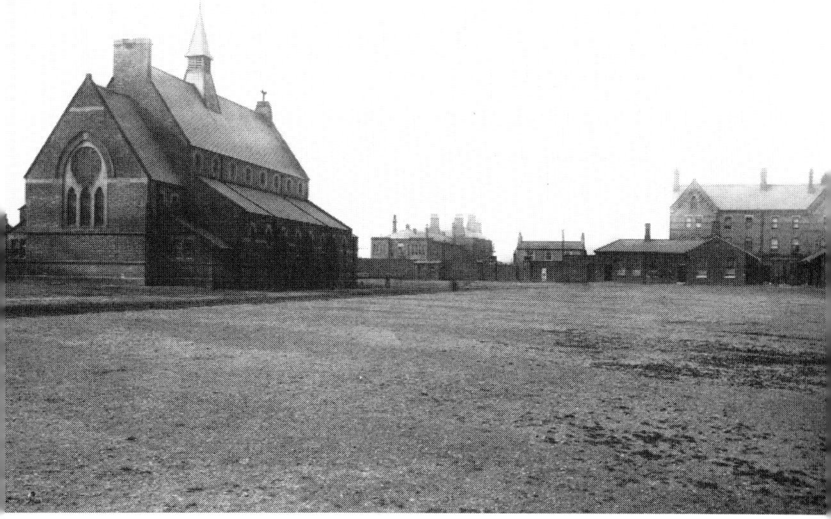

Gone from here are the men, horses, buildings and stables of the Royal Dragoon Guards. The site is now the Divisional Headquarters of the North Yorkshire Police. Only the church, which was known as the Garrison Church, remains, and it is now used by the police for storage. The other buildings were all demolished in the 1960s.

THE CAVALRY BARRACKS

THE CHURCH 1886 / 18720

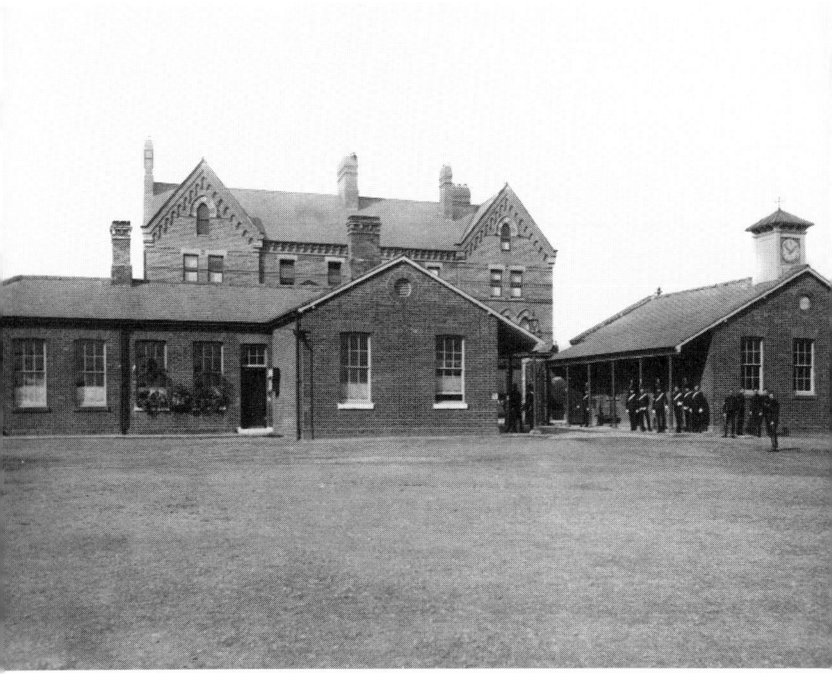

These barracks were built about three years after the Infantry Barracks, but the construction came under much criticism. There were no litter sheds, and horse manure was piled up under the men's room windows. Also, there were no proper urinals for the men to use at night. Not an attraction for new recruits! Thank goodness, these problems were eventually sorted out.

THE CAVALRY BARRACKS

MAIN GUARD 1886 / 18719

Watched over by their officers, the Royal Dragoons practice combat exercises using their swords. The regimental museum in Tower Street has displays of medals, uniforms and weapons, and models showing the battles that both this and other Yorkshire regiments fought in many parts of the world, including Egypt, Europe and the North-West Frontier.

THE CAVALRY BARRACKS

1886 / 18716

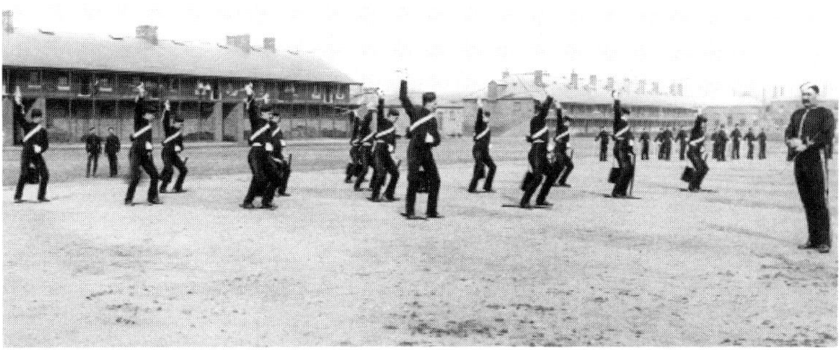

The smart uniformed soldier stands silent guard outside this building, built in 1878 on the corner of Fishergate and Melbourne Street. It is still used for offices, but no longer by the War Department. A horse must have recently passed by, as it has left a deposit on the side of the road.

THE WAR OFFICE

C1885 / 18468

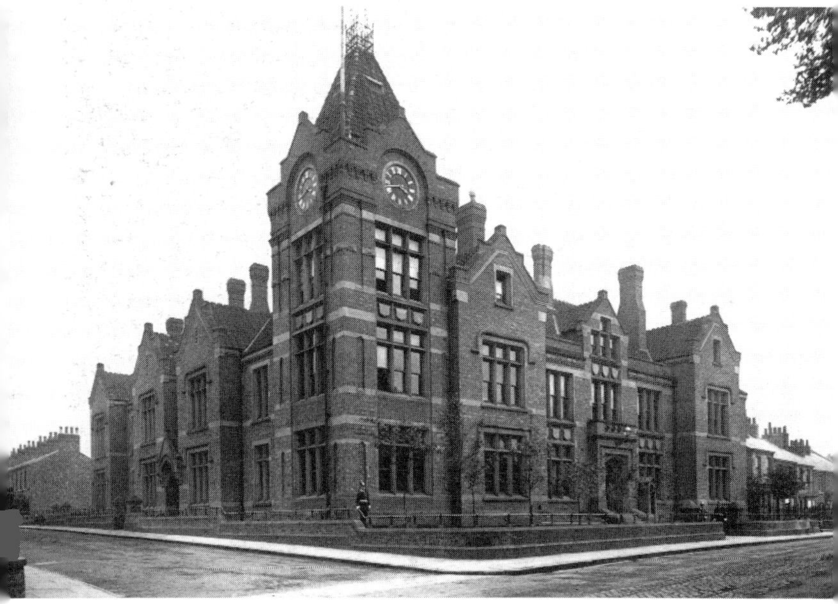

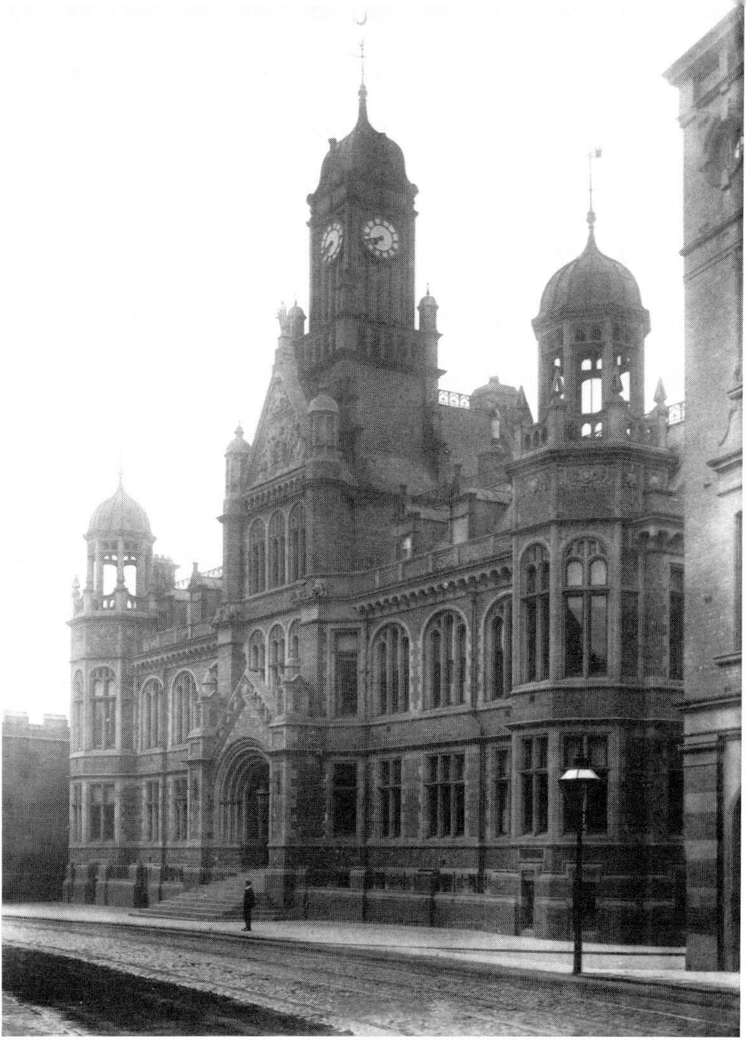

THE LAW COURTS
1893 / 32039

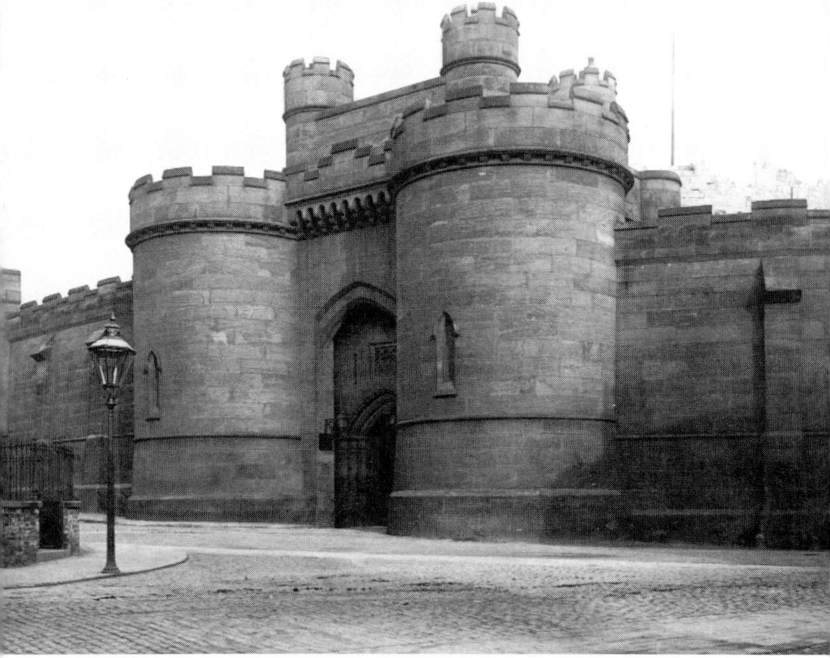

These awe-inspiring and formidable walls and gates were knocked down in 1934. At that time there were no conservation laws, and anything that was in the way of progress was destroyed. The walls once surrounded both the castle and Clifford's Tower. The site of the old gate is now a car park.

THE CASTLE GATE
c1885 / 18492

This was built in the 1770s; many notorious criminals were tried in York, including Dick Turpin in 1739. The area is known as the Eye of Yorkshire, or the Eye of the Ridings. Parliamentary elections were held here until the 19th century. Two of the courts are still used on a daily basis.

YORK CASTLE

ASSIZE COURT c1885 / 18497

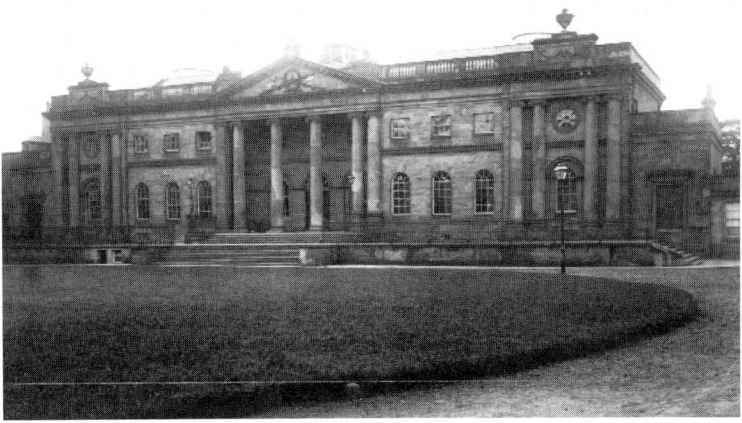

When Dick Turpin was arrested and tried it was for horse stealing, although his crimes included robbery and murder. He was using the name of Palmer, and it was not until he was imprisoned that his true identity was discovered. He was taken from the prison and hung at Tyburn gallows at Knavesmire, now the site of the York Racetrack.

YORK CASTLE

THE OLD PRISON c1885 / 18493

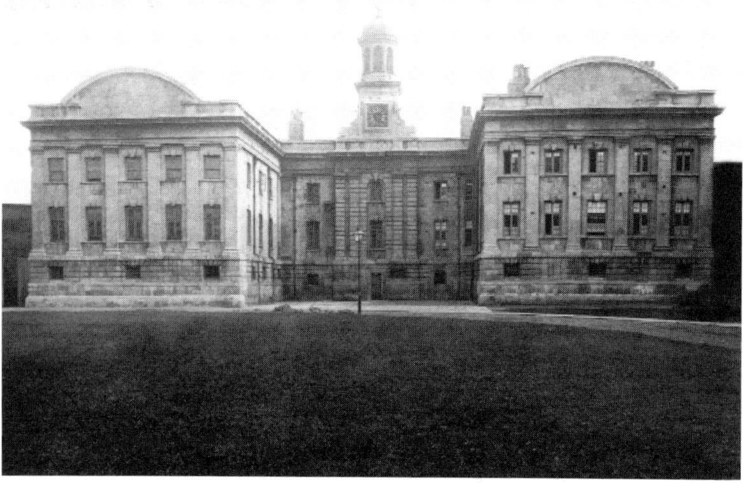

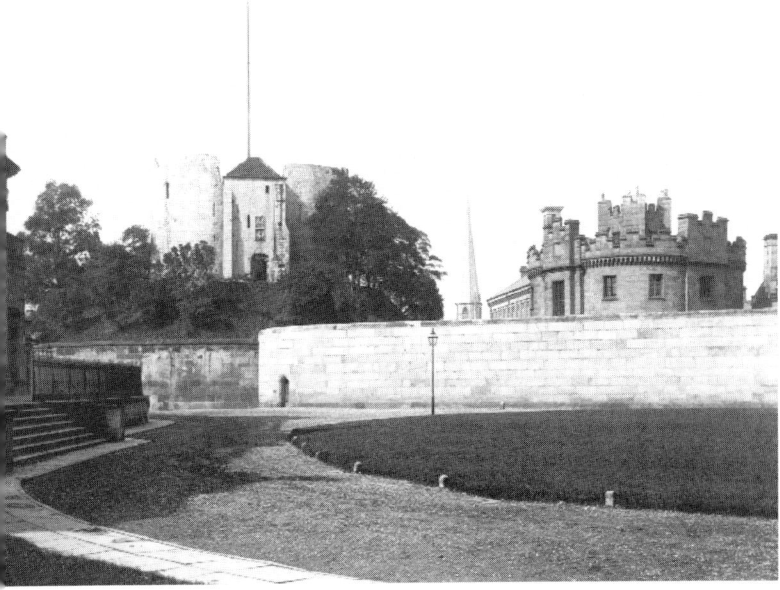

Panoramic views of the city can be seen from the top of this tower, which was built in the 12th century to replace a previous wooden castle. The arms that can be seen on the gatehouse are of Henry Clifford, Earl of Cumberland. Above the gatehouse there is a chapel.

CLIFFORD'S TOWER

1885 / 18488

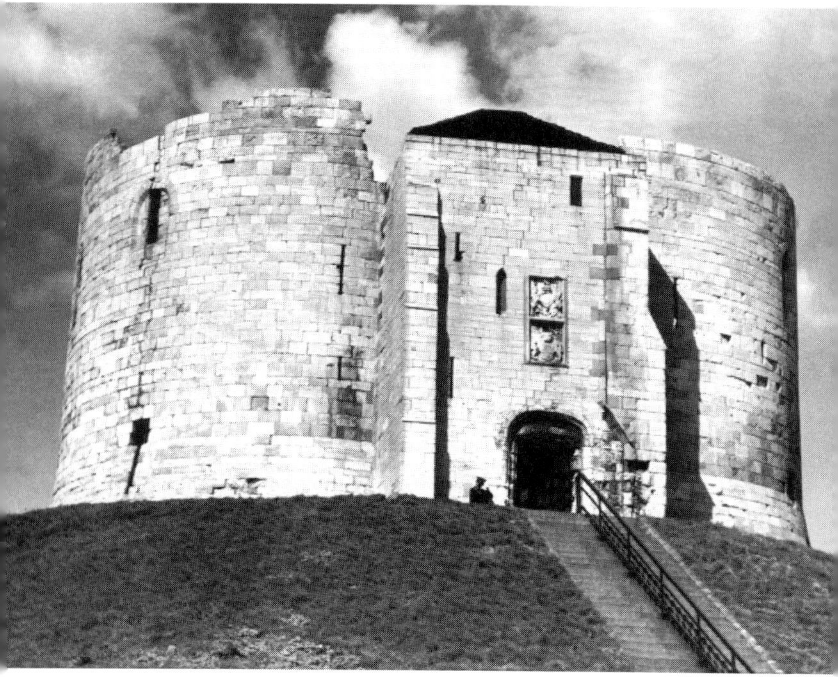

Built on a motte which is about 48 feet high, the tower itself is just over 33 feet high. In the 16th century Robert Redhead, a gaoler, wanted to demolish the tower, but the people of York and the Corporation decided it should be kept as a treasure second only to the Minster.

CLIFFORD'S TOWER

C1950 / Y12018

The land was acquired by the City Corporation in 1934 at a cost of £8,000. The Debtors' Prison was opened as a museum, which was then extended to the Women's Prison building. Amongst many other attractions, the museum has a reconstruction of a Victorian shopping street. Thousands of people flock here annually to this, one of the best-known museums in Britain.

THE CASTLE MUSEUM

C1955 / Y12037

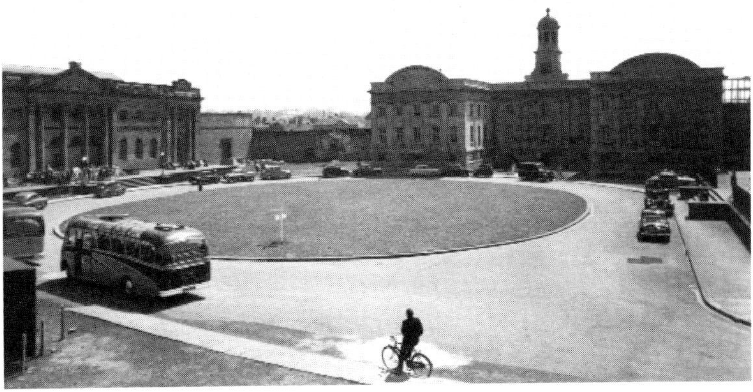

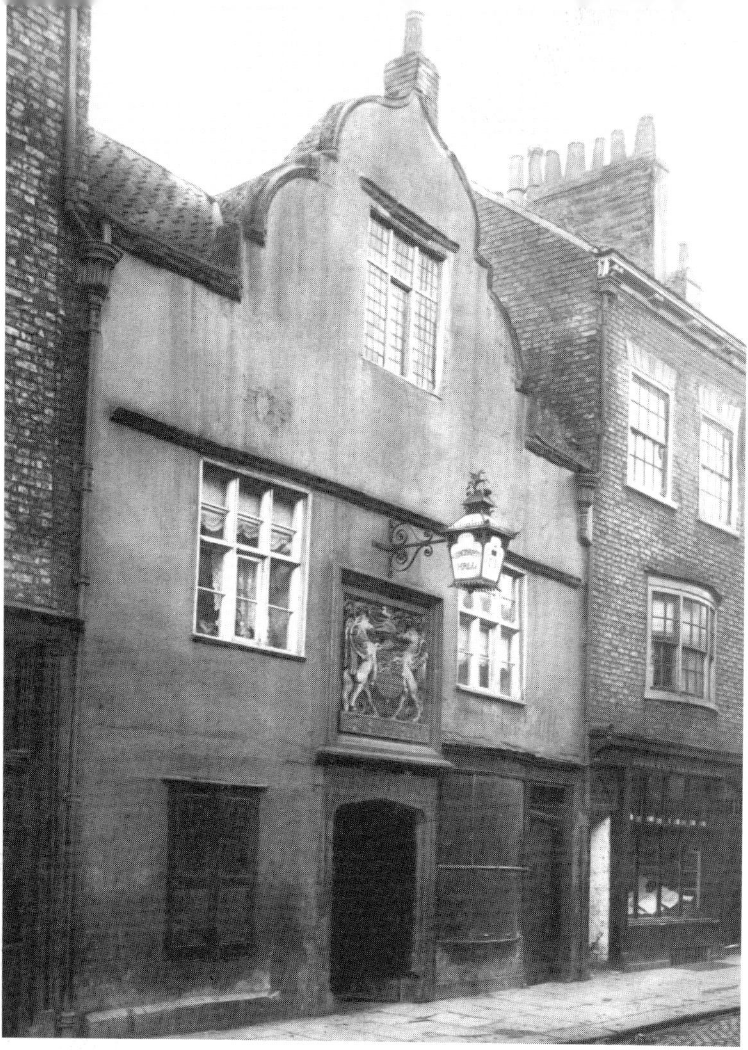

THE MERCHANT ADVENTURERS' HALL
1892 / 30635

Viewed here from the Fossgate entrance, the hall is the largest timber-framed building in York; the undercroft is the oldest part. The chapel, which was rebuilt in 1411, still retains part of the original 15th-century oak screen and a 17th-century pulpit.

THE MERCHANT ADVENTURERS' HALL

1909 / 61851

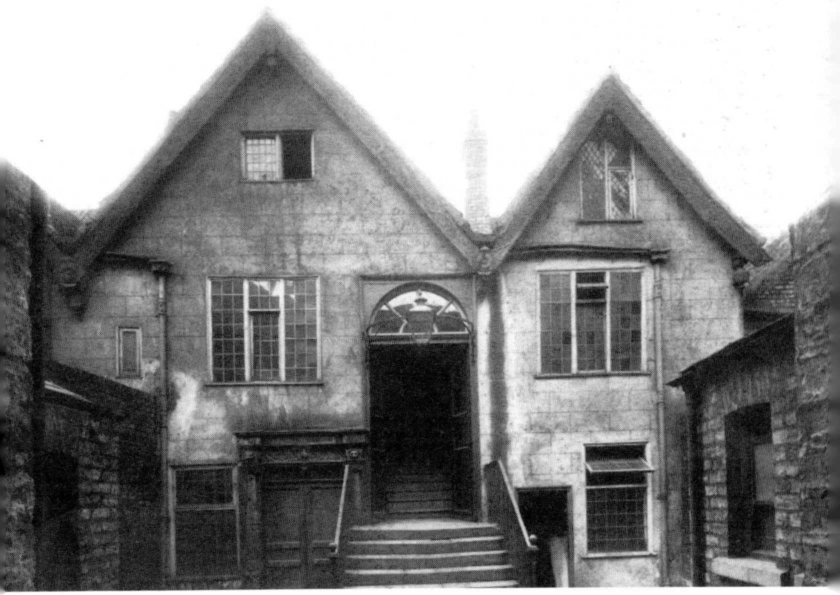

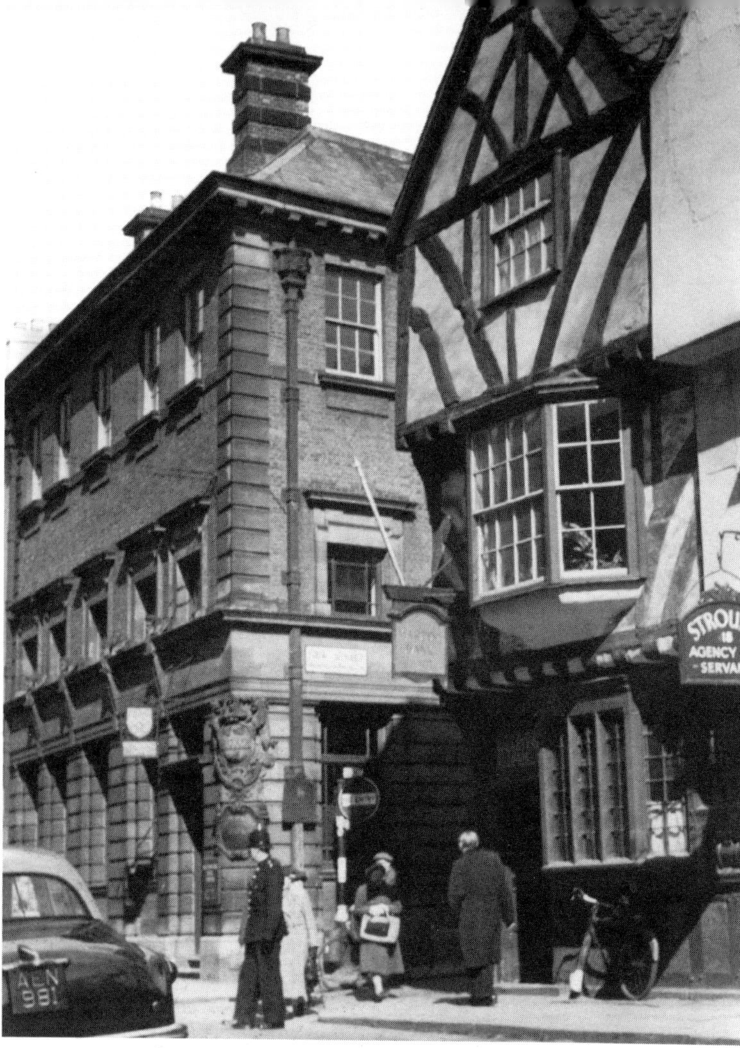

A TUDOR HOUSE

c1950 / Y12011

This is the second Station Hotel; it was completed in 1878. Renamed the Royal York Hotel when it was bought in 1983, it is a Grade 2 listed building. The station and hotel were designed by Thomas Prosser. Both thrive to the present day. The first hotel, built about 1851, still stands to the east of the old railway station, and is used by British Rail as offices.

THE STATION HOTEL

C1885 / 18434

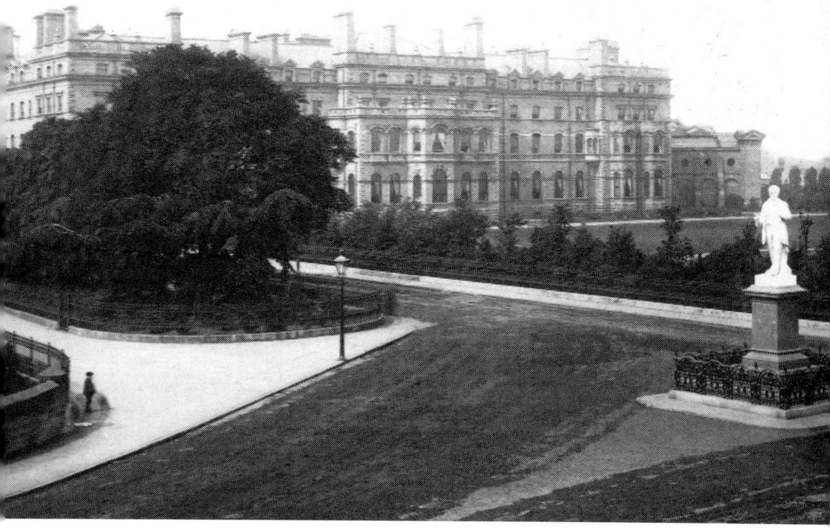

The new station was built to replace the original station that had been completed in 1841. Construction took place between 1873 and 1877 on the site of a Roman cemetery. When it was completed, it was said to be the largest station in the world. Here, to the left, the roof top can be seen; inside it sweeps in a wonderful curve above the main platforms.

THE STATION AND THE HOTEL

1907 / 58687

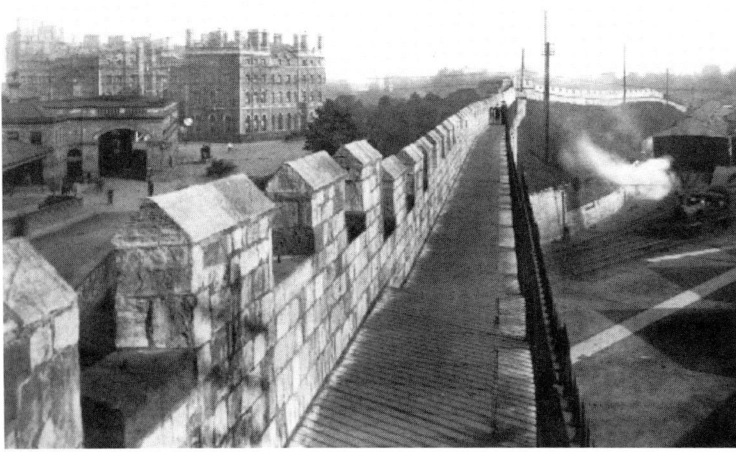

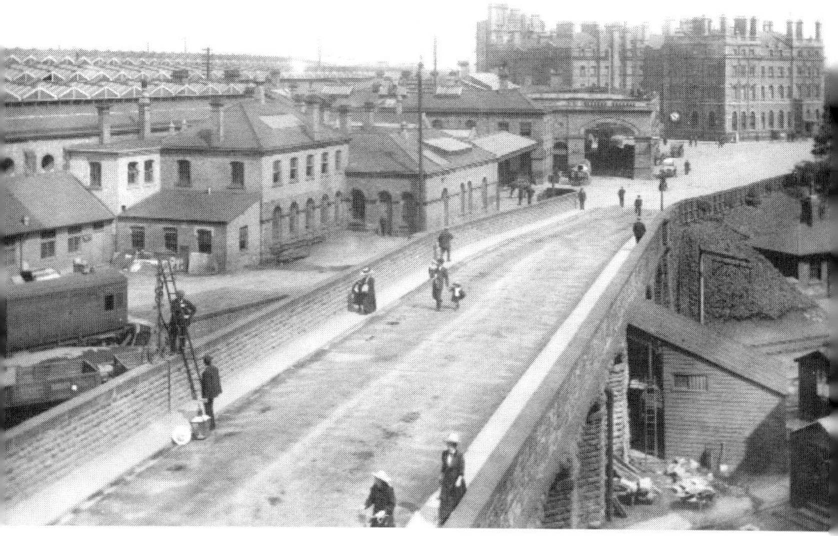

When the second station was constructed, new openings had to be made in the walls to give better access, because it was just outside the city walls. Much of the street plan was changed. One example was that Thieves Lane became Station Road.

THE STATION AND THE HOTEL
1909 / 61849

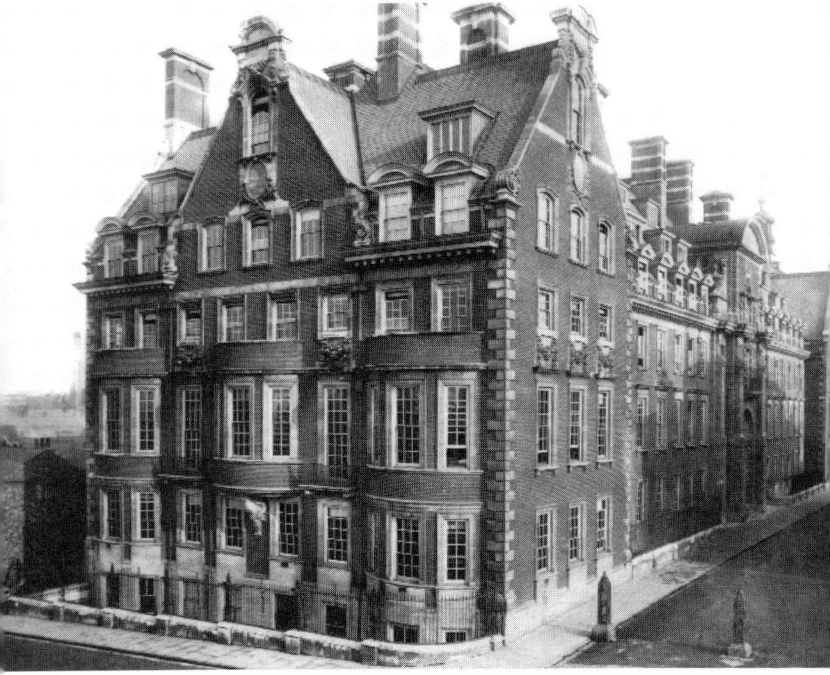

This is the headquarters of British Rail Eastern Region, situated in Station Road. When this photograph was taken, the building had just been completed. Many different architectural styles were used, including Dutch gables. The badges on the building are of three different railway networks.

THE NORTH-EASTERN OFFICES

1907 / 58689

This view shows the rear of the Assize Court. The whole area has changed almost beyond recognition. The castle walls to the right of the view are now demolished. The cannon is no longer there, and the monument, although still in almost the same place, now stands in the middle of a roundabout on a busy road.
It commemorates the fallen soldiers in the Boer war of Alexandra, The Princess of Wales' Own Yorkshire Regiment.

THE WAR MONUMENT

1909 / 61719

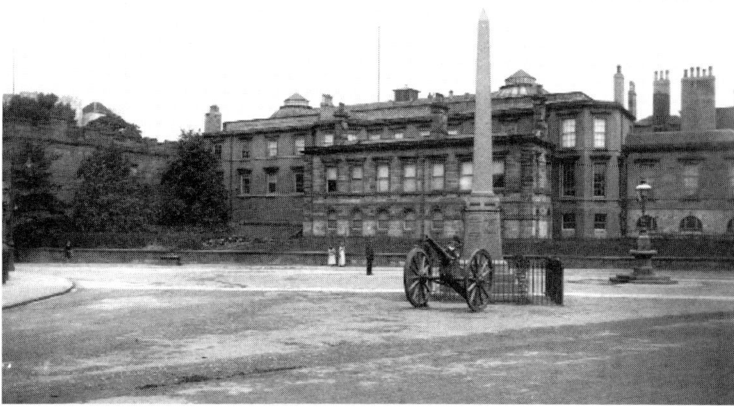

Over the centuries, the hall had been attacked by death watch beetle. Repairs began, but when in 1942 they were almost complete, the hall was bombed and very badly damaged. In the 1950s the hall was rebuilt as near to the original design as possible. Each of the pillars in the main hall are from a single oak tree donated by the county families of Yorkshire.

THE GUILDHALL

C1885 / 18461

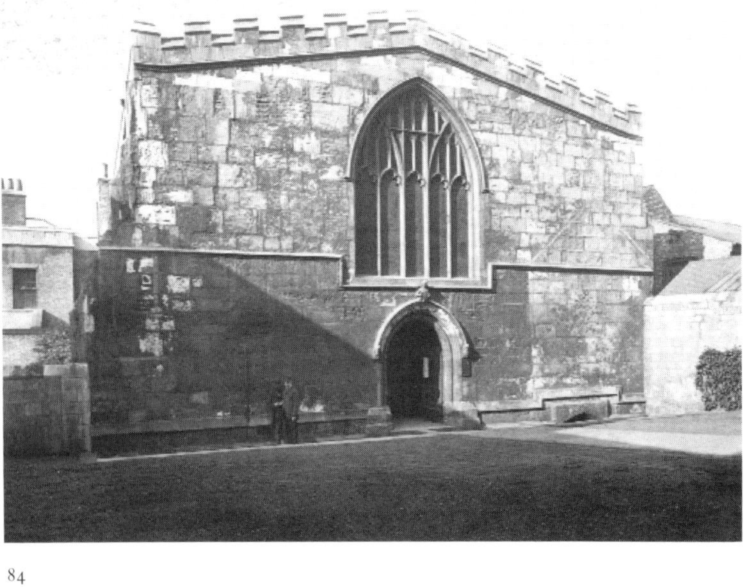

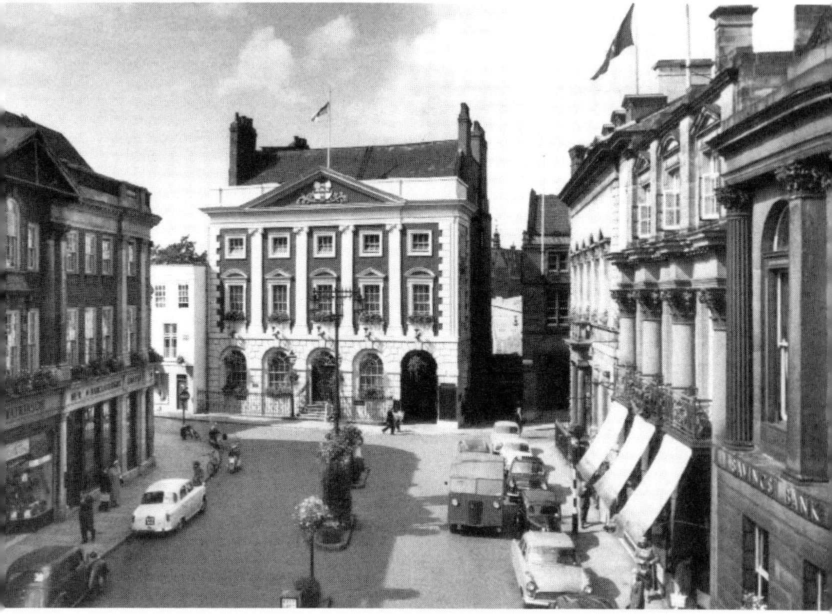

In St Helen's Square, what had been a Guildhall Chapel and then a public house was demolished to make way for the building of a residence for the Lord Mayor. The result was this charming abode. It was built in about 1775, and is now one of the three oldest surviving buildings of its kind in England.

THE MANSION HOUSE

C1955 / Y12048

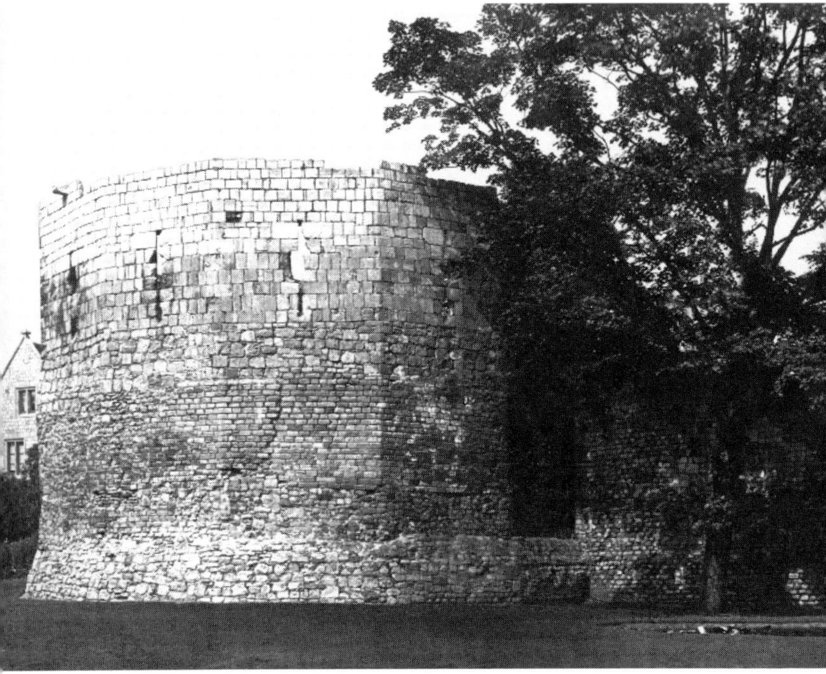

The lower part of this strange structure is Roman; it was the west corner of the Roman fort. The upper part is 14th-century. Inside, there is a small ruined tower. When this stretch of the wall was excavated, the archaeologists found that the ramparts dated from Roman, Saxon, Viking, Norman and medieval times, and that the earth bank grew with each occupation.

THE MULTIANGULAR TOWER

c1885 / 18485

Near the River Ouse, situated in what is now the Museum Gardens, this building was the guest house for St Mary's Abbey. The ground floor was built in the early 14th century, while the timber-framed first floor was added in 1420; a new roof was built in the 1930s.

THE HOSPITIUM

C1885 / 18483

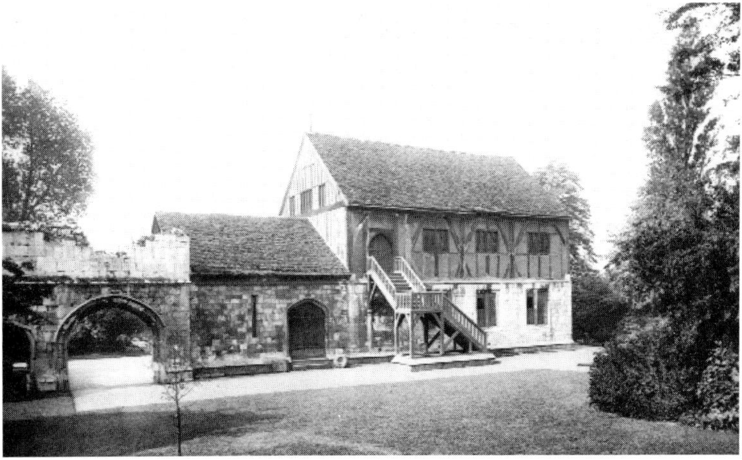

Built around 1280 for the Abbot of St Mary's Abbey, the building was enlarged in the 15th century. Although belonging to the King, and known as the King's Manor, it was never used as a royal residence. It is now owned by the University of York, and parts are open to the public, including the impressive Huntingdon Room built by the Earl of Huntingdon.

THE ANCIENT PALACE OF THE STUART KINGS

1909 / 61720

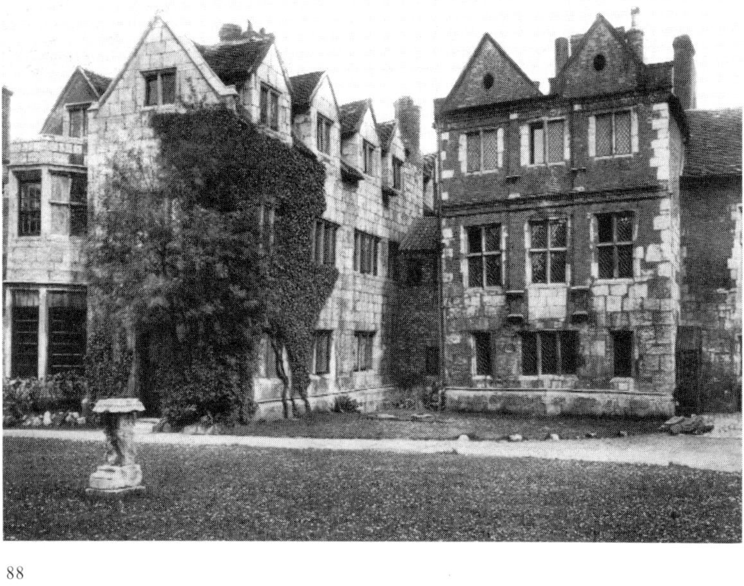

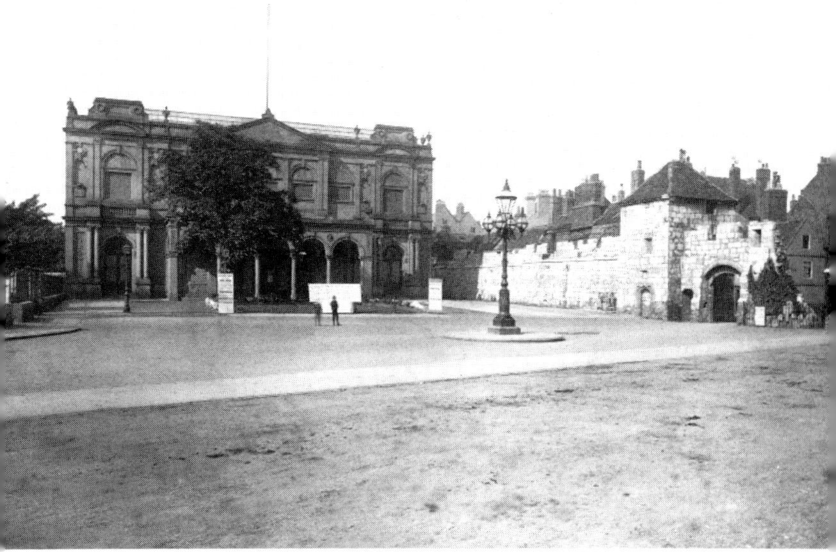

An exhibition of fine art was held in the grounds of Bootham Park Hospital in 1866. It attracted thousands of people, so it was decided that a permanent building for further exhibitions should be erected. This building, in what became known as Exhibition Square, opened in 1879; it is now the York City Art Gallery.

THE EXHIBITION

C1885 / 18466

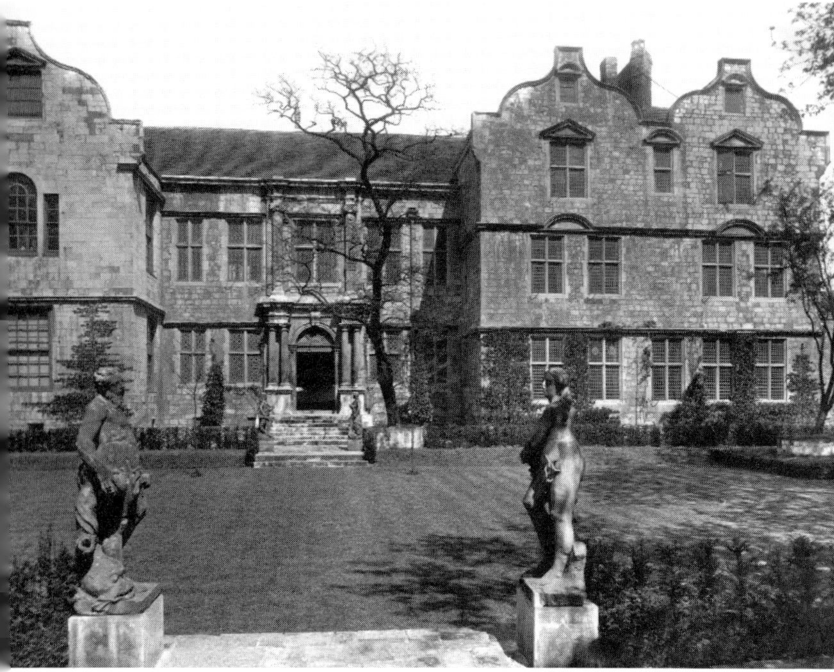

In this, the most interesting of all the houses in York, a young apprentice plumber stated that while he was working in the cellar, he heard a trumpet playing; then he saw an army of Roman soldiers marching, but as if on their knees. When the cellar floor was dug up, the remains of a Roman road was discovered where the soldiers' feet would have been!

THE TREASURER'S HOUSE

1908 / 59796

The college was first built for the Minster's Chantry Priests in about 1465. These priests had plenty of money and plenty of time on their hands, and were always getting up to mischief. It was decided to house them somewhere so that they could be close to the Minster, but out of the way of trouble.

ST WILLIAM'S COLLEGE

1892 / 30634

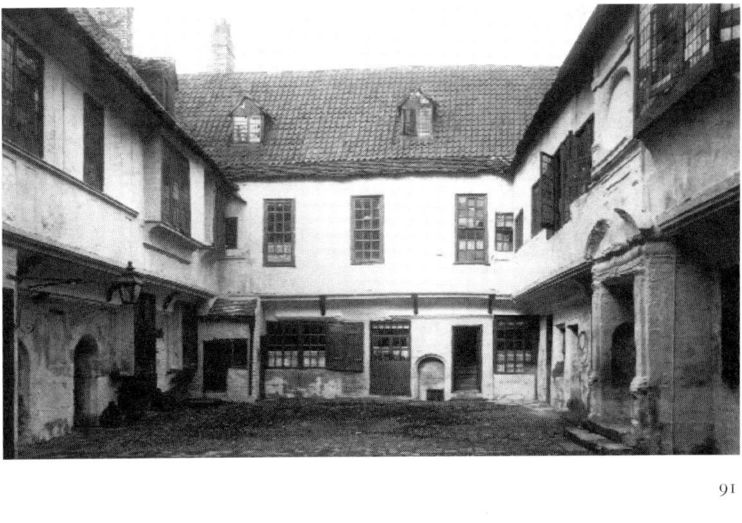

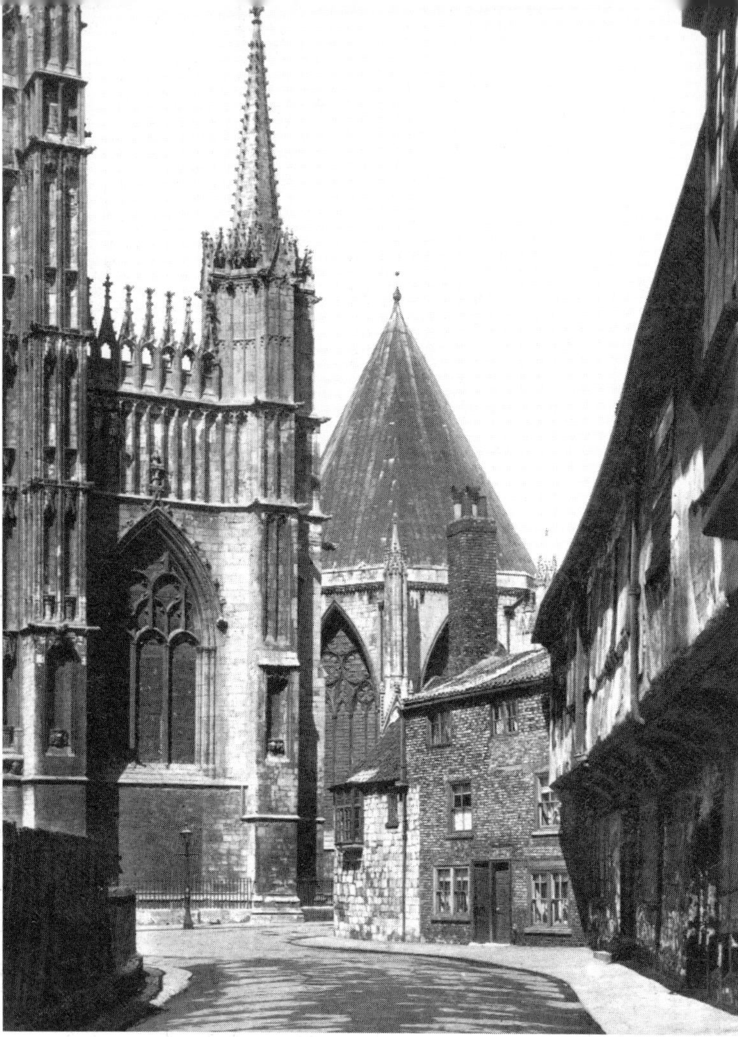

ST WILLIAM'S COLLEGE

1908 / 59795

The building was named after William Fitzherbert, who was the great-grandson of William the Conqueror. At the turn of the 19th century, the building was used as tenements. The Convocation of York eventually bought the property; they used it as a meeting place until the amalgamation with the Church of England.

ST WILLIAM'S COLLEGE

1909 / 61852

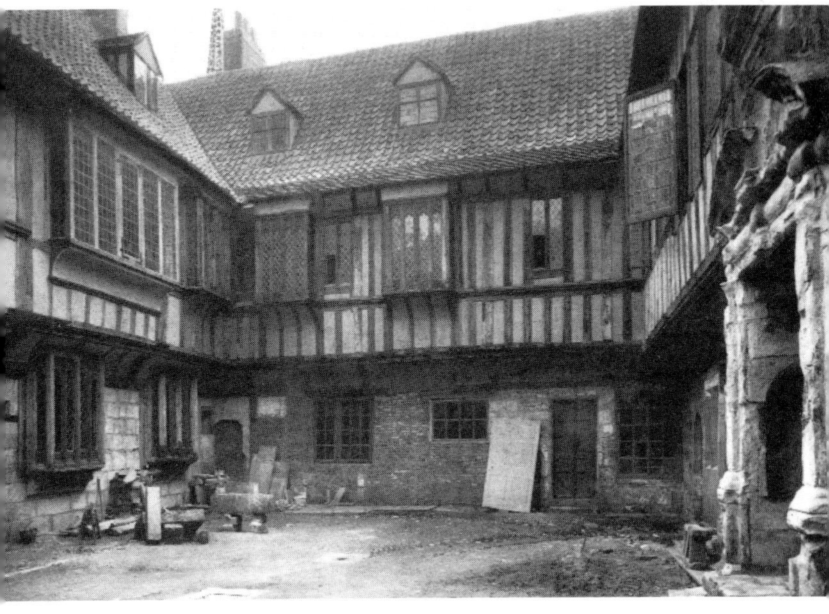

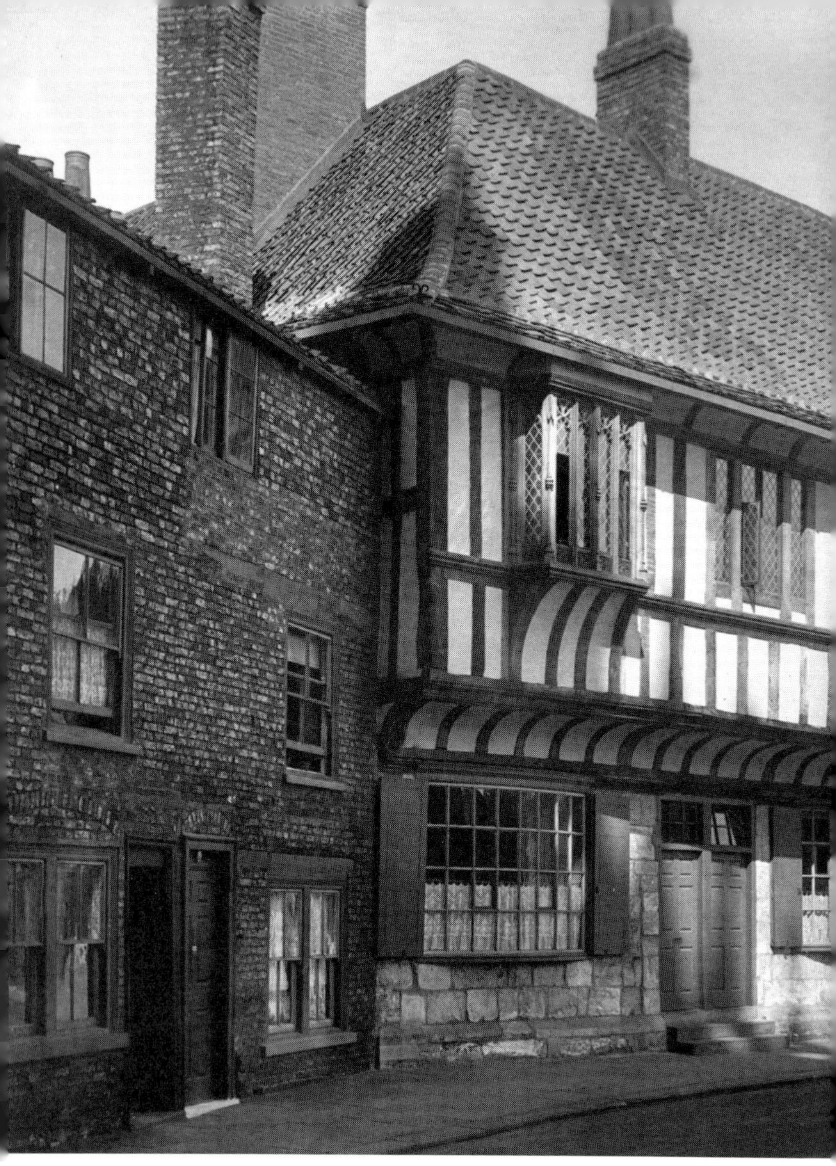

ST WILLIAM'S COLLEGE

1911 / 63600

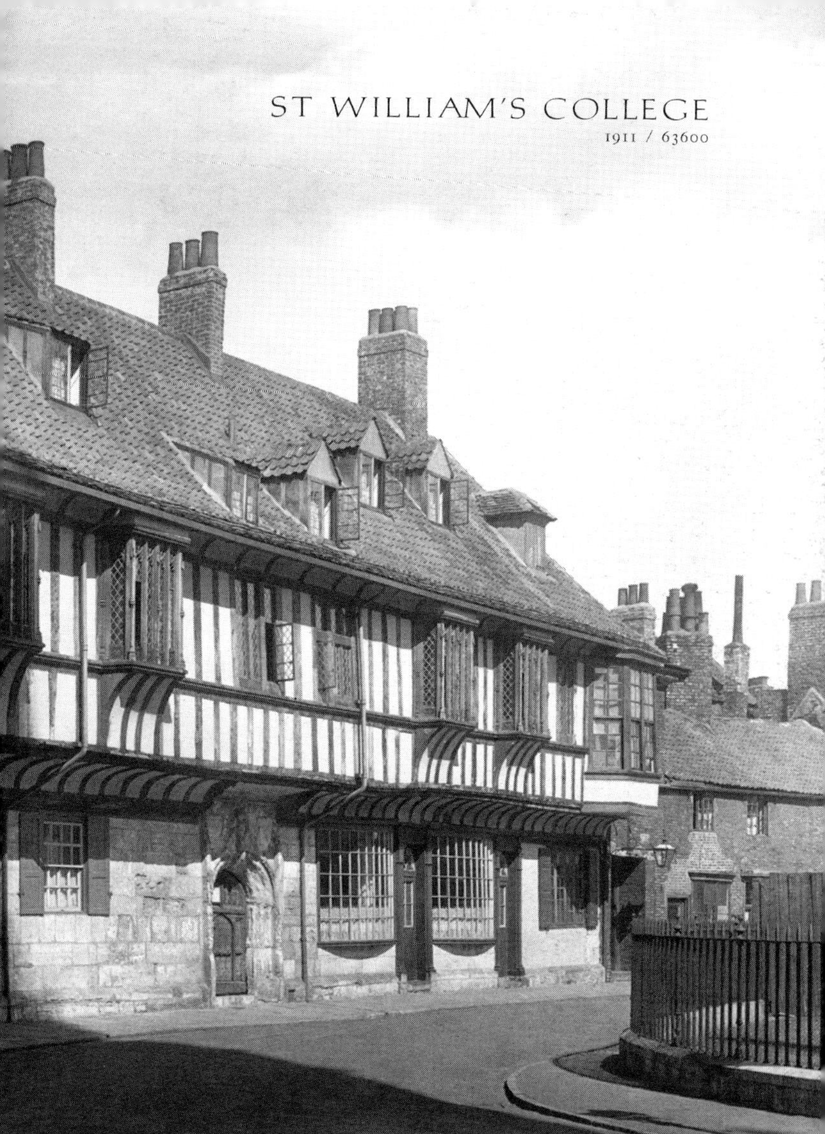

Photograph No 61852 shows neglect, but now, a few years later, there have been improvements. The interior quadrangular courtyard is entered from College Street through an arched gateway. Above the entrance is a stone figure of St William (the Archbishop of York) who died in 1154. Nowadays the courtyard is well-cared-for.

ST WILLIAM'S COLLEGE

1920 / 69602

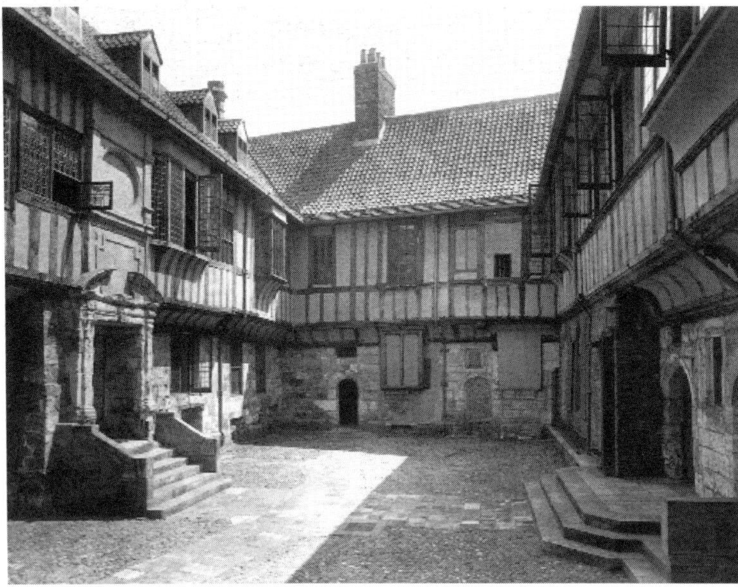

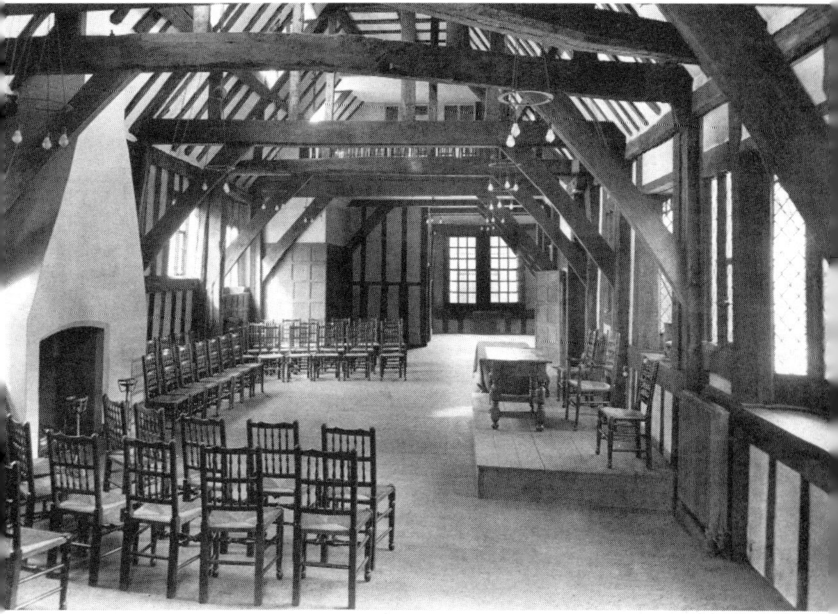

Two brothers who rented rooms here robbed and murdered a cleric. The younger brother hid in a chest with the booty, but was found and hung after his older brother gave him away. The older brother, although free, was haunted by guilt and died quite young. It is said that his footsteps can still be heard at night pacing the upper floors.

ST WILLIAM'S COLLEGE

THE LAYMAN'S ROOM 1911 / 63606

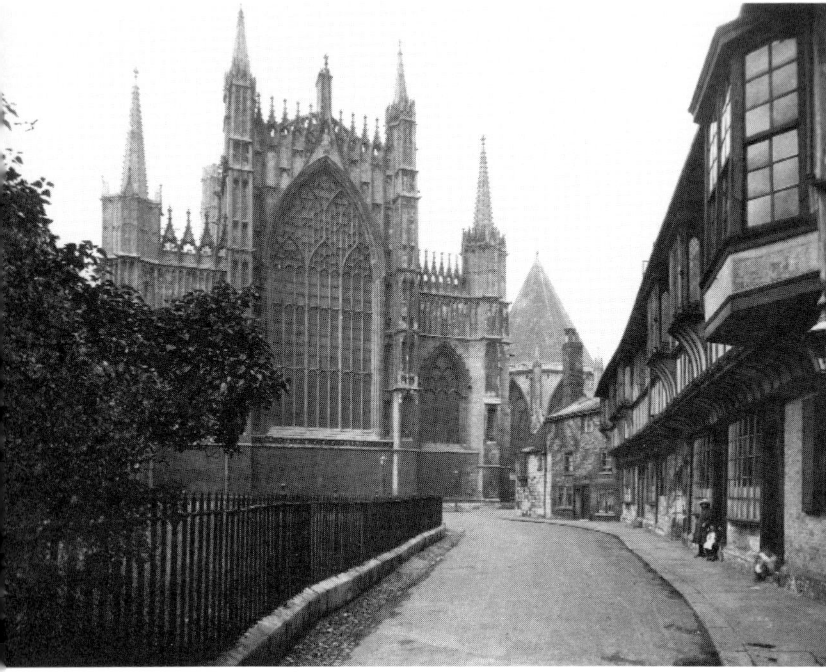

As we can see, it was just a hop and a skip for the chantry priests to reach the Minster from their dwellings. At the time of this scene, the building would have been tenements. The children on the steps seem fascinated by the photographer.

THE MINSTER

THE EAST END AND ST WILLIAM'S COLLEGE 1913 / 65443

The central doors, which can just be seen in this photograph, were made by the famous wood carver, Thompson of Kilburn: his signature, a mouse, is carved on the right-hand door. The College is now open to the public as a restaurant and exhibition hall.

ST WILLIAM'S COLLEGE

C1950 / Y12014

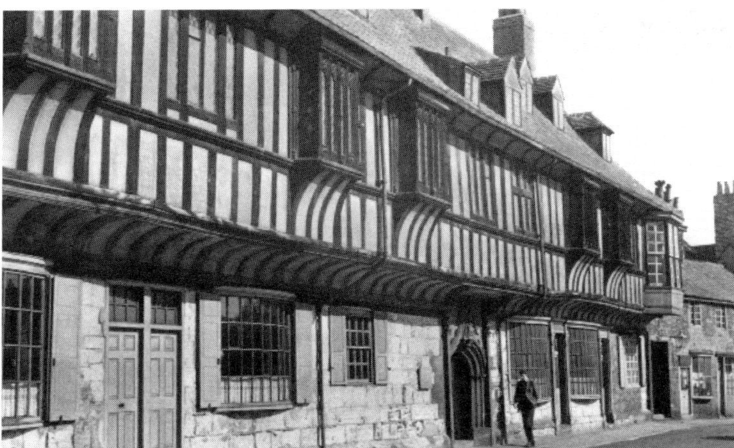

The original building was built as a small private school in 1838. In 1844 it was acquired by the Dean and Chapter to use for St Peter's School, which had outgrown its former site. It is now the oldest public school in England. The architecture of the building is mainly Gothic revival.

CLIFTON

ST PETER'S SCHOOL 1909 / 61724

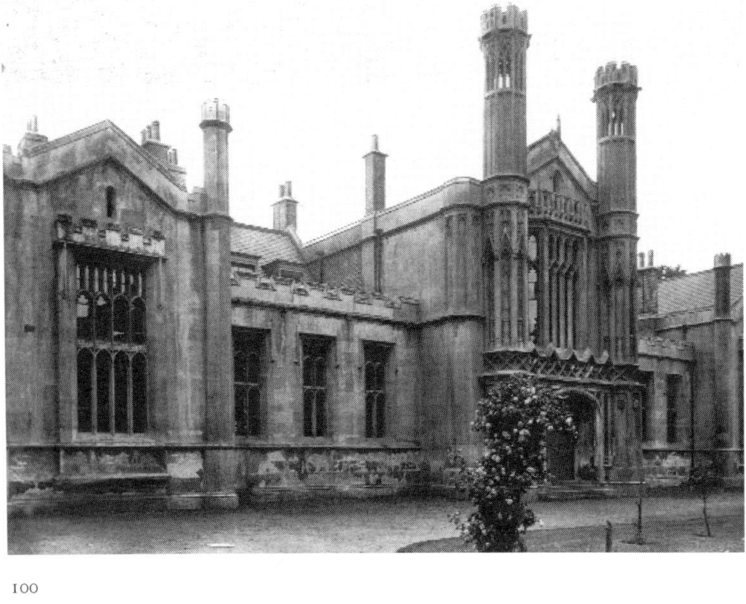

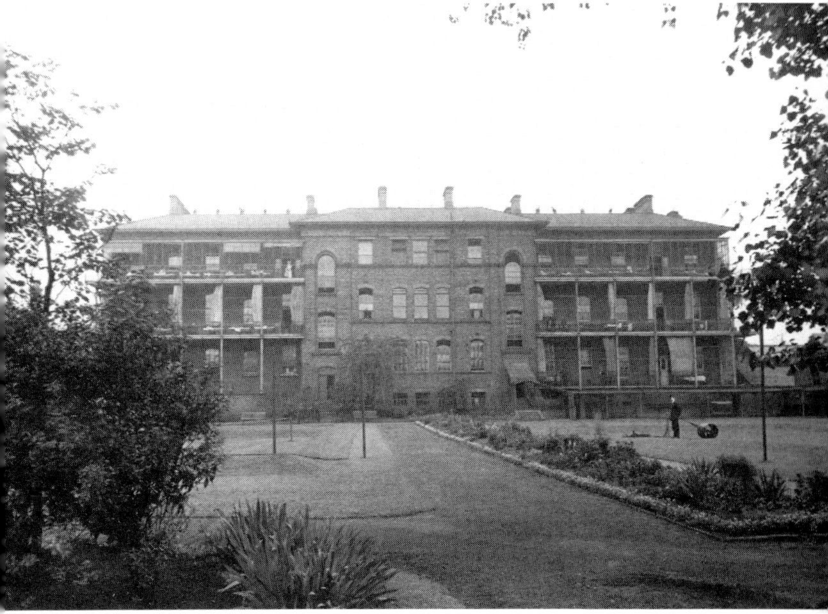

The hospital was founded in 1749 and rebuilt in 1850. This building eventually closed as a hospital and became offices for the water board. For the last few years it has been used as flats. The area to the right is now a Sainsbury's supermarket. Here the gardener can be seen having a respite from his toil to stand and watch the photographer.

THE COUNTY HOSPITAL

1913 / 65463

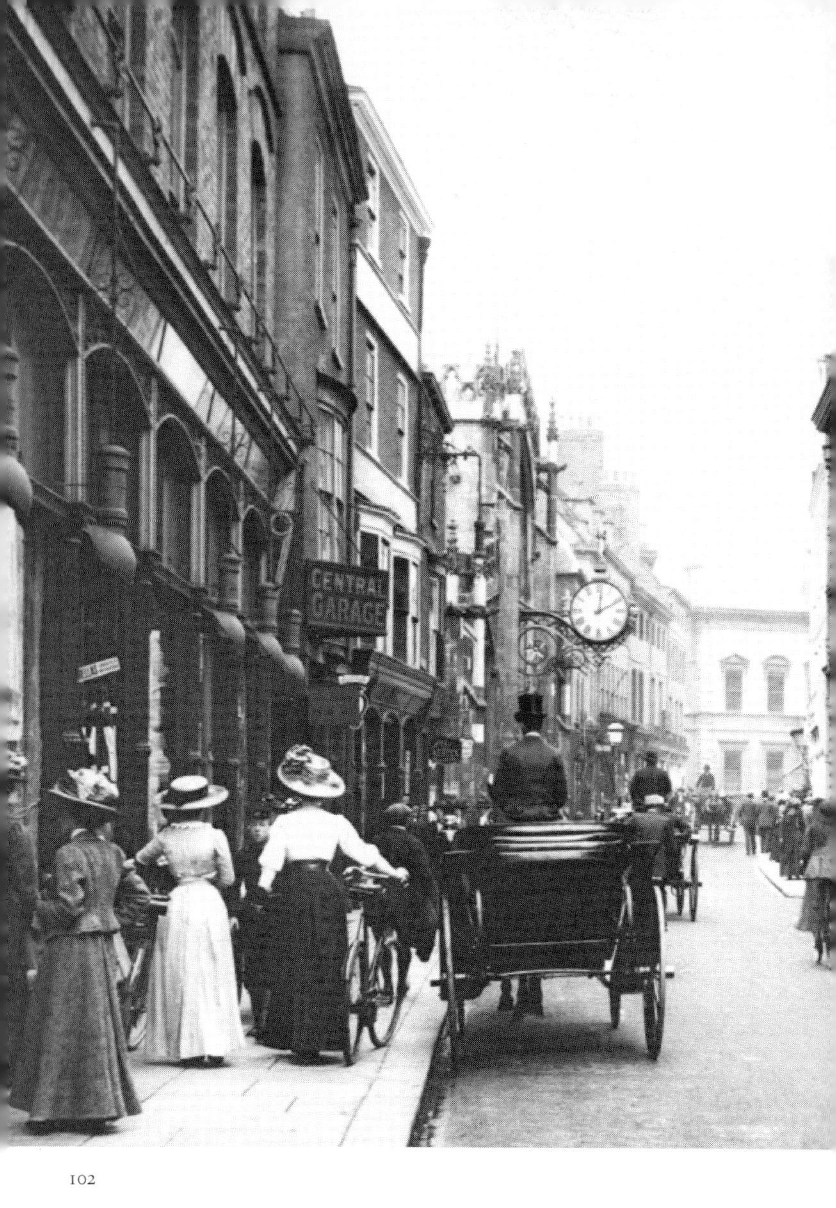
CENTRAL
GARAGE

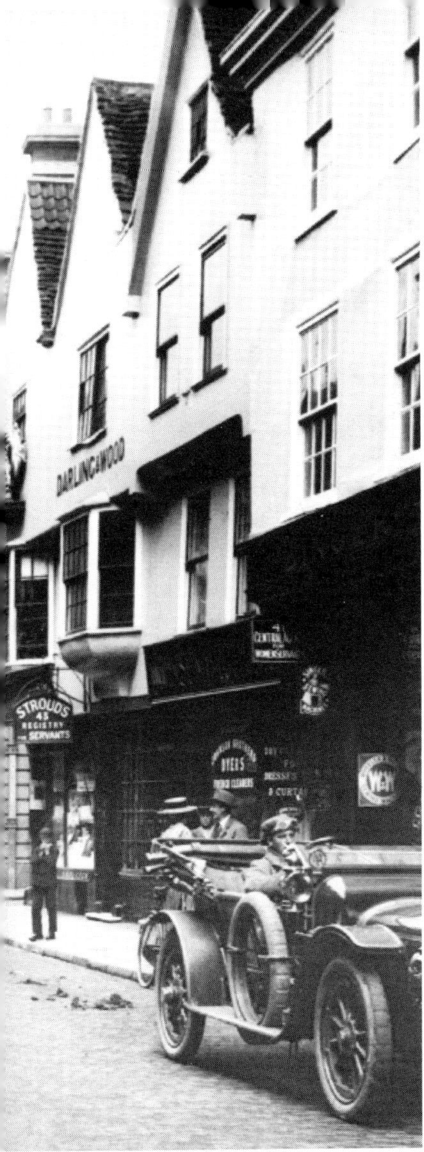

In the 1920s, the owner of a chain of grocery stores had two carved cats placed on the upper front of his shop - they were supposed to frighten the rats away from the river bank. The large clock on its ornamental bracket outside St Martin's Church dates from 1668; it still shows present-day shoppers the time. The chap in the smart motor car looks a proper toff!

CONEY STREET

1909 / 61723

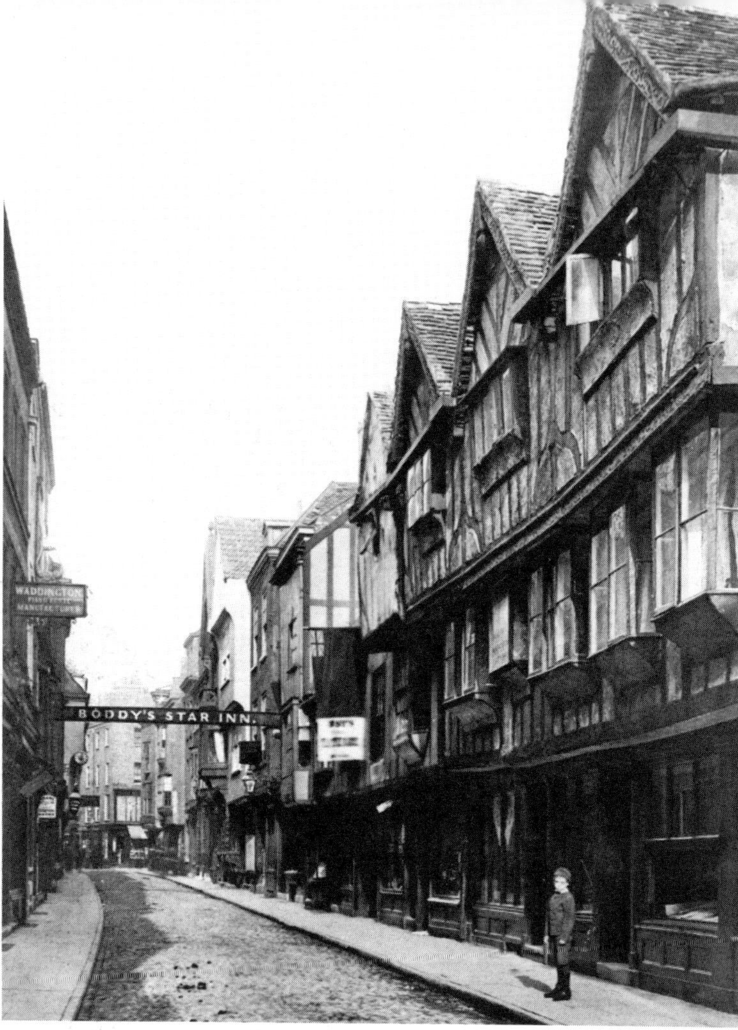

STONEGATE
1886 / 18449

Here the wording on the banner has been changed to 'Ye Olde Starre Inne'. Once there would have been many of these gallows signs, as they are called, but this is the only one remaining in York. Sometimes the signs would hang so low that people would have to duck to pass by. The 17th-century inn has survived, but it has been totally altered.

STONEGATE
c1960 / Y12055

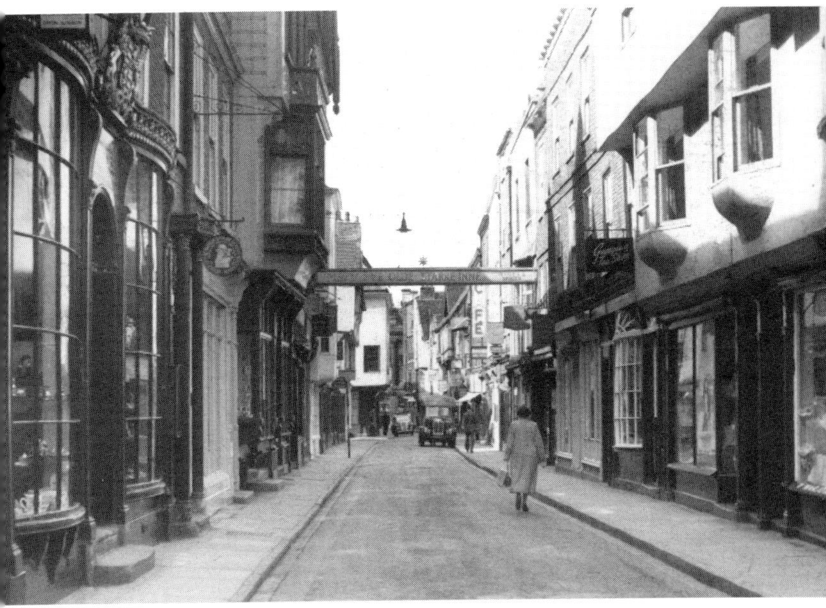

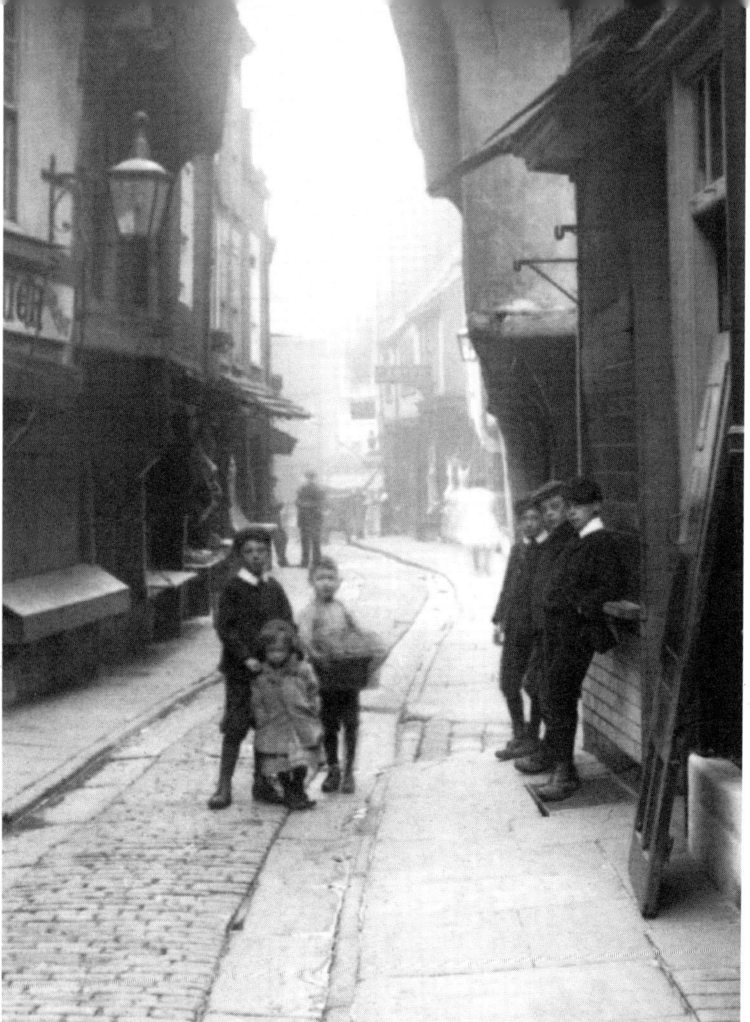

THE SHAMBLES

1909 / 61722

This crowded scene shows the stalls sited on Parliament Street and into St Sampson's Square. The market was moved to nearby Newgate in 1955. At the forefront to the left of the photograph is a horse-drawn bus with baskets of wares being carried on the roof. The age of the motor car was just dawning.

THE MARKET

1908 / 59799

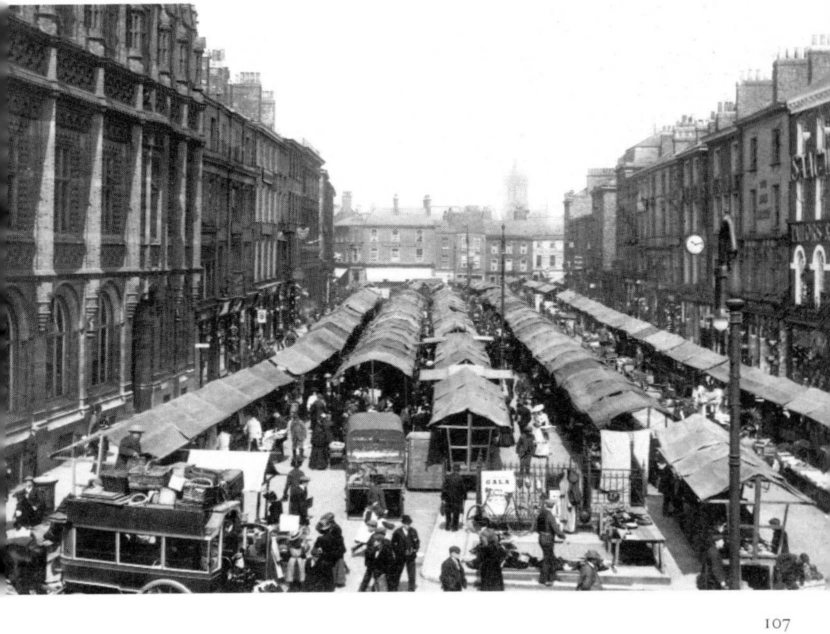

The Shambles was originally known as Haymongergate, because it was the site of the haymarket. Hay was used to feed the animals awaiting slaughter; it was illegal to graze livestock within six miles of the city centre. The street is very narrow, and at one point outstretched hands can touch each other from the opposite sides of the upper storeys.

THE SHAMBLES
c1962 / Y12062

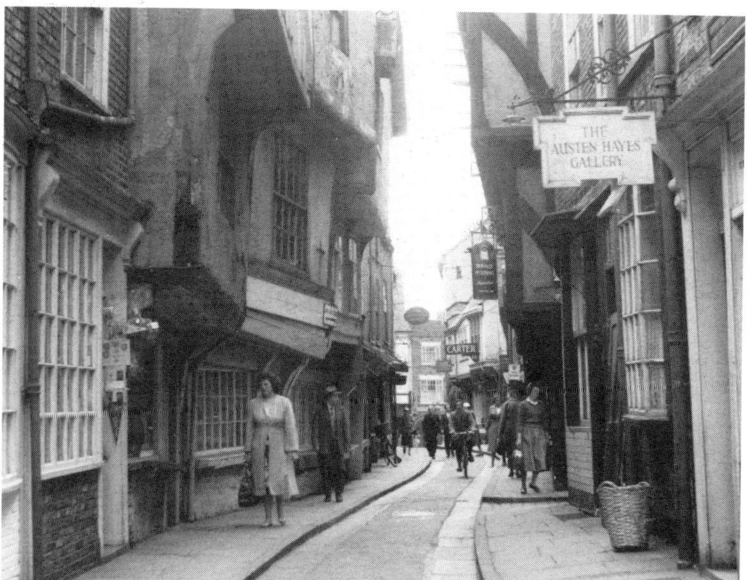

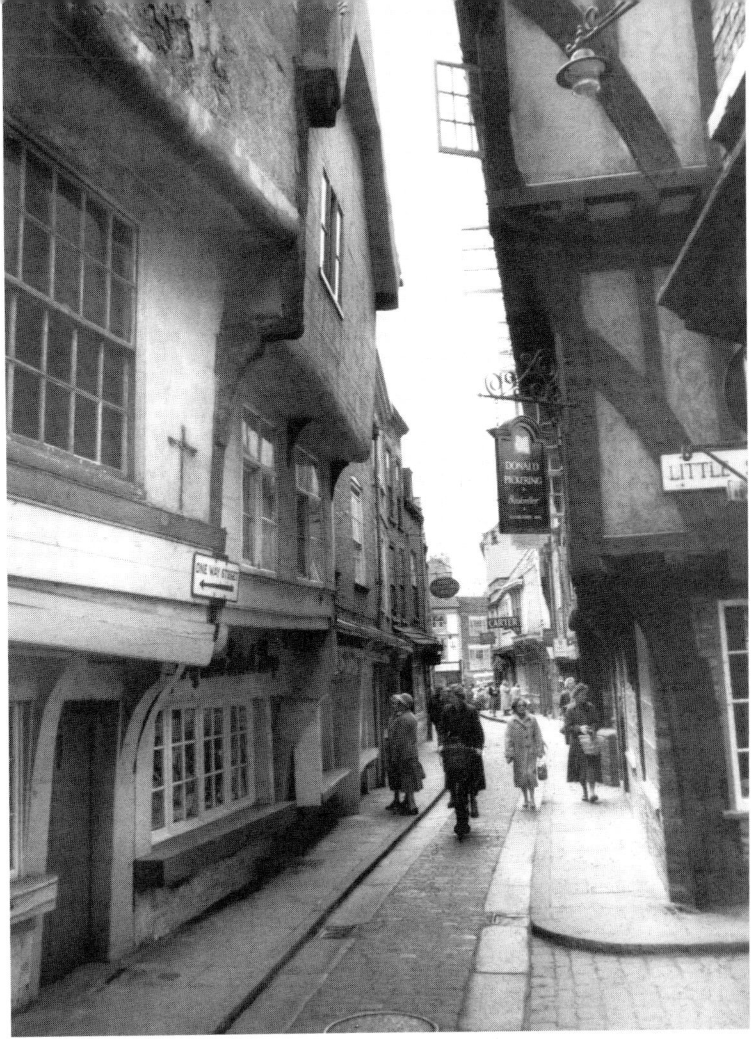

THE SHAMBLES
c1960 / Y12071

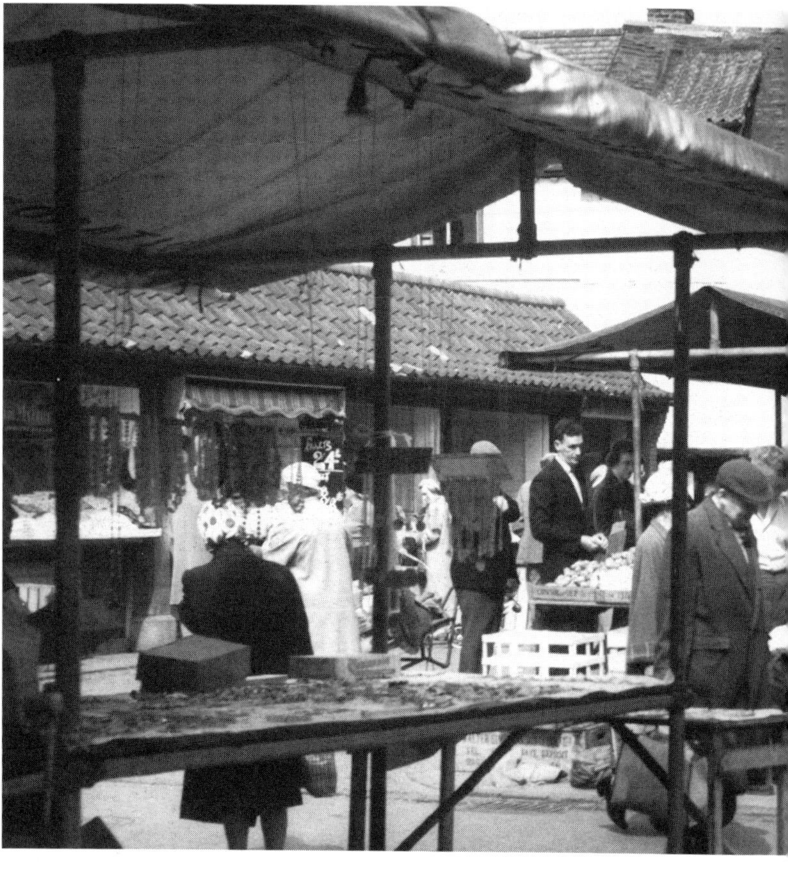

LITTLE SHAMBLES

MARKET c1960 / Y12063

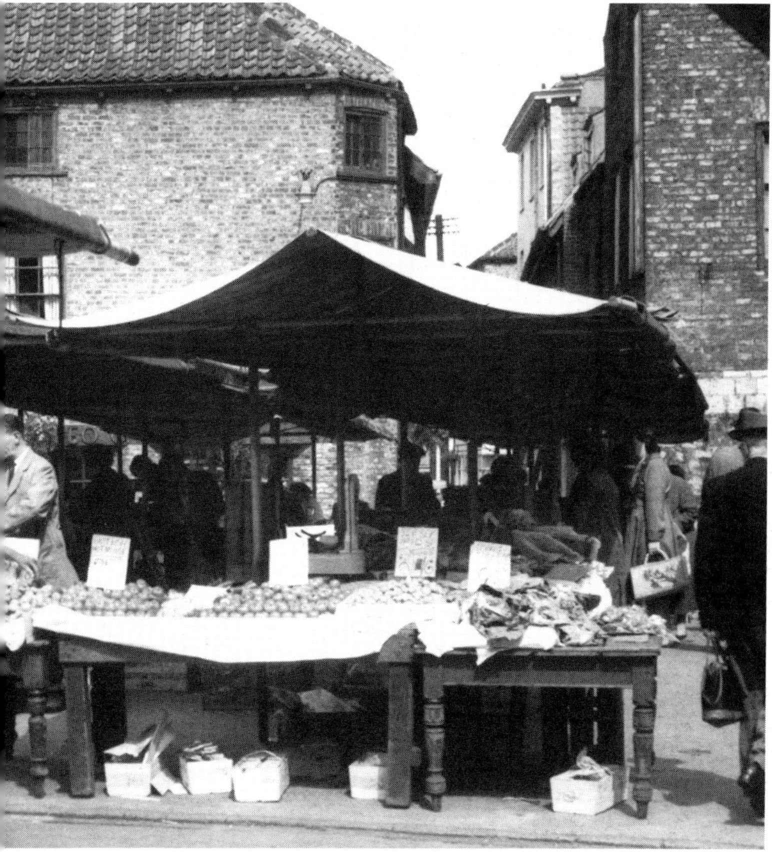

The wealthy Butchers' Guild once had a guildhall in this street; it was demolished in the 19th century. At the Pavement end of the street stood the town pillory - anyone found guilty of treason was beheaded here. Little Shambles is called so because it is only a few yards in length.

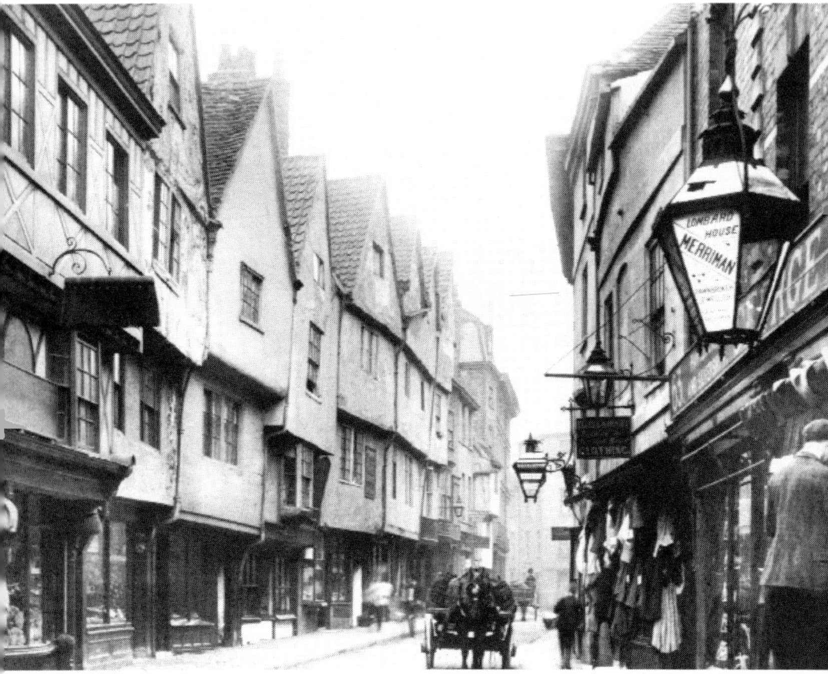

On the right is Merriman's Pawnbrokers, with its leaf-decorated lamp hanging above the shop front. On the left is a large sweeping brush head trade sign, now in the York Castle Museum: it advertised Seale's Brush and Mat Warehouse. The lamp to the forefront on the Londesbro Arms has now disappeared.

LOW PETERGATE

1892 / 30632

In this view, Seales Warehouse is now a toy shop, and next door is York's Pram and Nursery Furniture Centre. Perhaps the two gentlemen talking outside Merrimans have something to pawn!

LOW PETERGATE

C1950 / Y12006

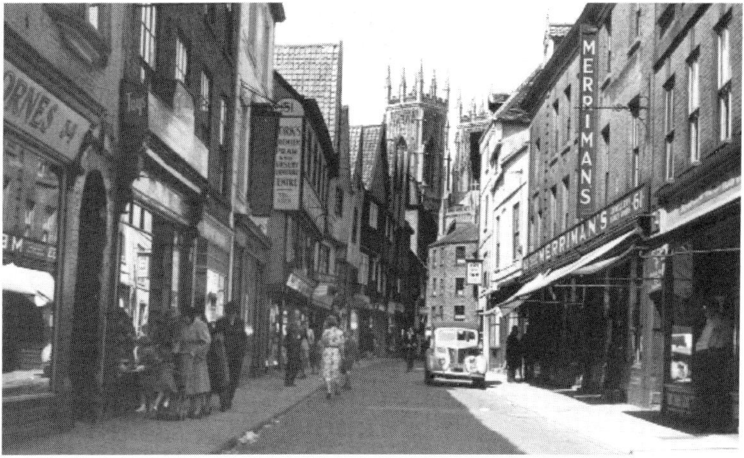

A carved wooden Indian holding a cigar still stands silent guard above one of the shop fronts in this street; it was once used to symbolise to the illiterate that the shop was a tobacconist. Scaffolding is in place on one of the Minster towers, as serious repairs were taking place.

LOW PETERGATE

c1960 / Y12061

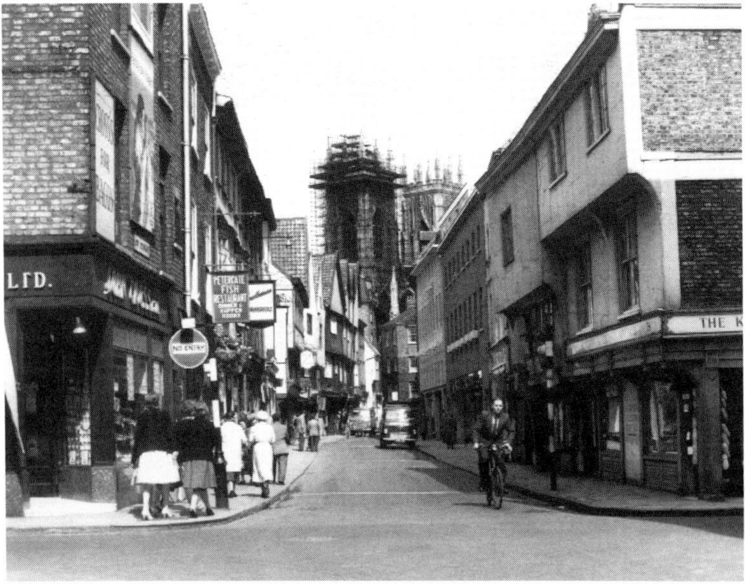

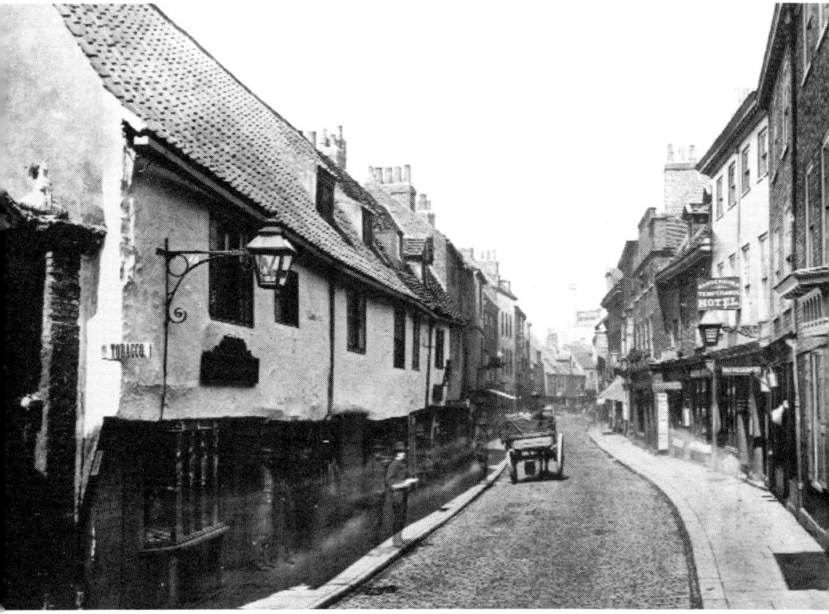

To the left of the street is a gate, erected in 1766, which leads to Holy Trinity Church. The houses here, on what is called Our Lady's Row, are amongst the oldest in England - they are early 14th-century. To the right of this view is the Sanderson's Temperance Hotel, now long gone. Shops now line this side of the street.

GOODRAMGATE
1886 / 3443

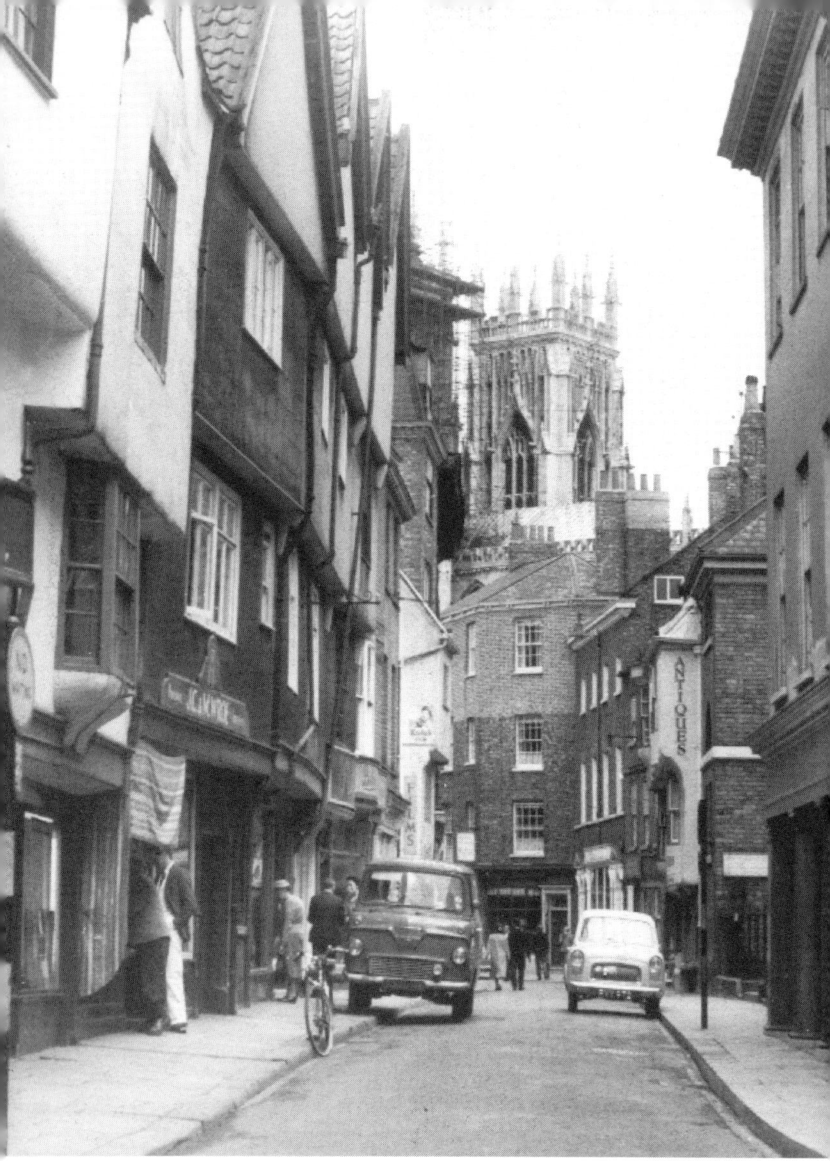
ANTIQUES

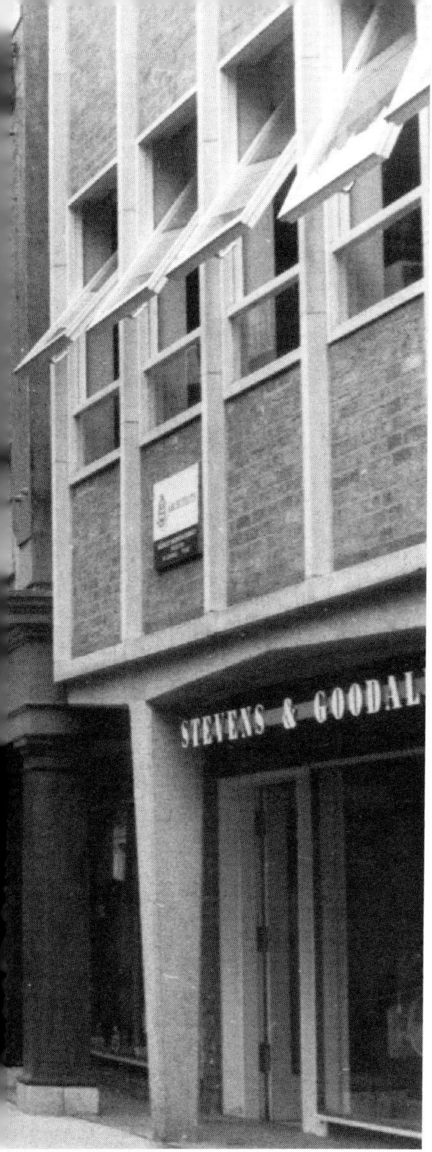

This view was taken from King's Square. The street was originally part of the Roman city's main road, or Via Principalis. The pawnbroker has gone; instead there is a modern shopping block housing the furniture shop of Stevens and Goodall.

LOW PETERGATE

C1960 / Y12060

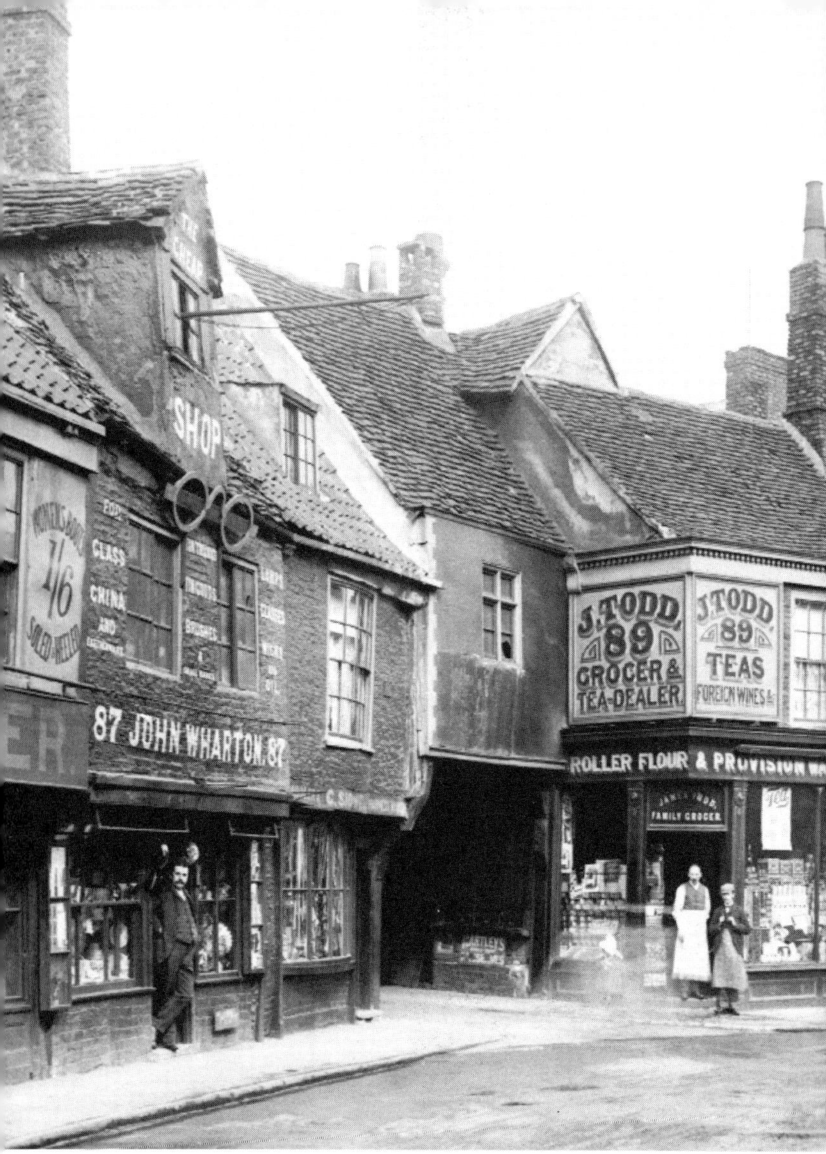
SHOP
GLASS
CHINA
AND
1/6
87 JOHN WHARTON 87
J. TODD
89
GROCER &
TEA-DEALER
J. TODD
89
TEAS
FOREIGN WINES &c
ROLLER FLOUR & PROVISION
FAMILY GROCER

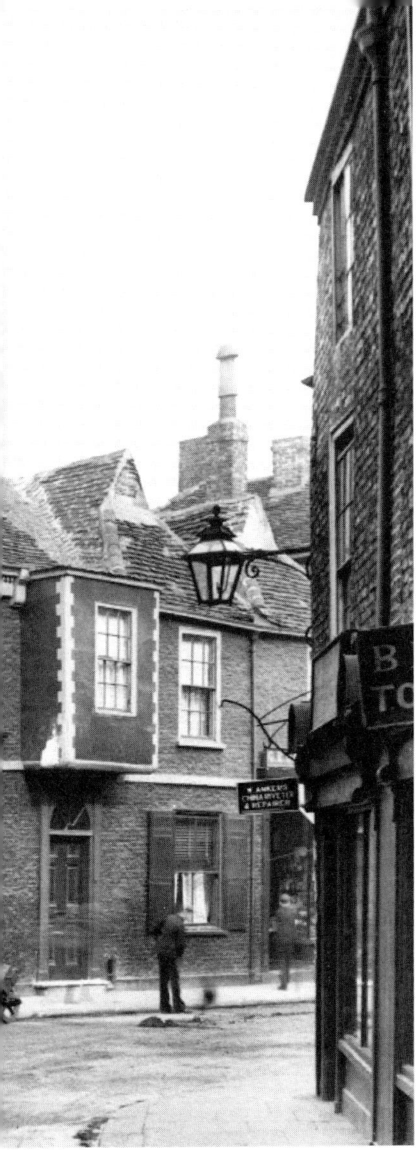

The covered way at the side of J Todd's Grocer and Tea Dealer was built for the vicars-choral, so that they could cross from where they lived in Bedern to the Minster Yard without being molested. The grocer's became an office for the National Trust in 1903. It was situated where College Street joins Goodramgate on the eastern side.

GOODRAMGATE
1892 / 30631

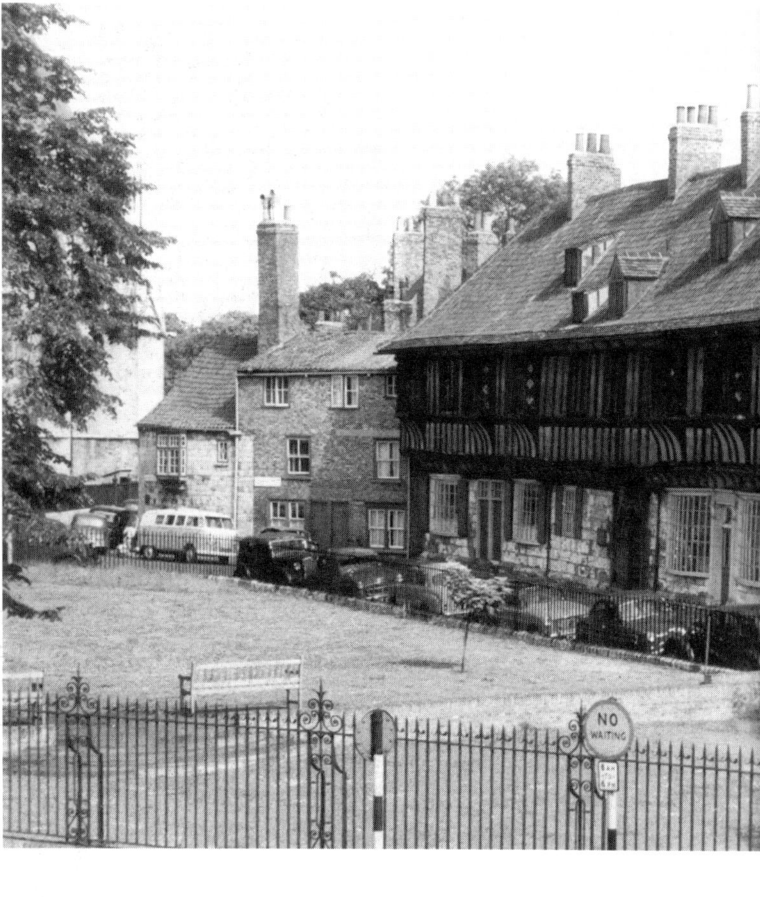

COLLEGE STREET
c1960 / Y12053

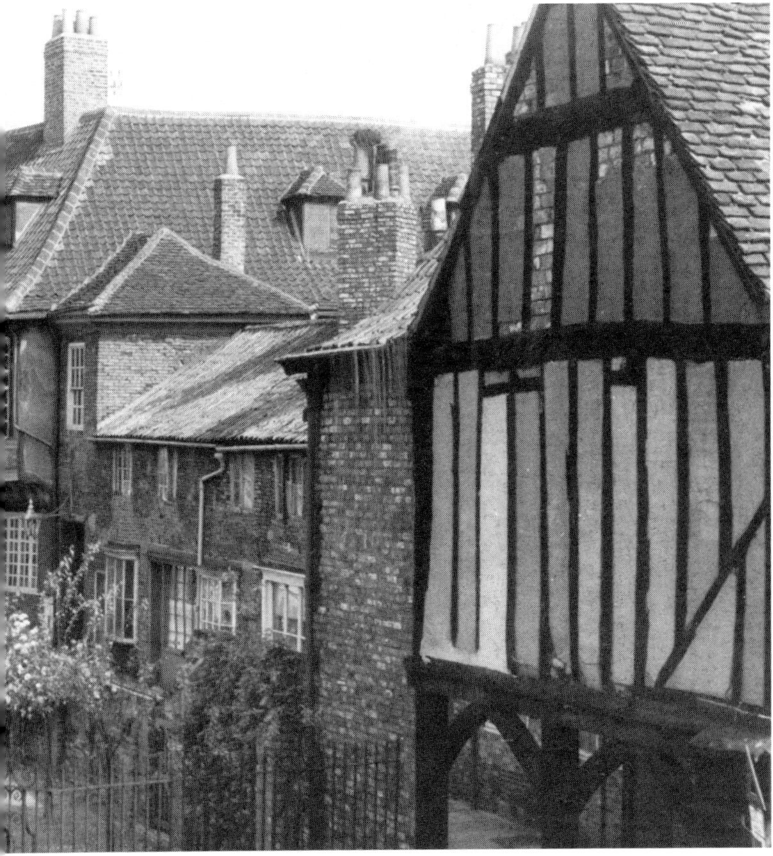

Once known as Vicar's Lane and then Little Alice Lane, the street branches off to Minster Yard, where the Theatre Royal opened in 1730 - it was the first theatre in York. The road to the front of the houses is now much wider, and there is a small park opposite the college.

INDEX

PLEASE HELP US BRING FRITH'S PHOTOGRAPHS TO LIFE

Our authors do their best to recount the history of the places they write about. They give insights into how particular towns and villages developed, they describe the architecture of streets and buildings, and they discuss the lives of famous people who lived there. But however knowledgeable our authors are, the story they tell is necessarily incomplete.

Frith's photographs are so much more than plain historical documents. They are living proofs of the flow of human life down the generations. They show real people at real moments in history; and each of those people is the son or daughter of someone, the brother or sister, aunt or uncle, grandfather or grandmother of someone else. All of them lived, worked and played in the streets depicted in Frith's photographs.

We would be grateful if you would tell us about the many places shown in our photographs—the streets with their buildings, shops, businesses and industries. Describe your own memories of life in those streets: what it was like growing up there, who ran the local shop and what shopping was like years ago; if your workplace is shown tell us about your working day and what the building is used for now. With your help more and more Frith photographs can be brought to life, and vital memories preserved for posterity.

We will gradually add your comments and stories to the archive for the benefit of historians of the future. Wherever possible, we will try to include some of your comments in future editions of our books. Moreover, if you spot errors in dates, titles or other facts, please let us know, because our archive records are not always completely accurate—they rely on 150 years of human endeavour and hand-compiled records.

So please write, fax or email us with your stories and memories. Thank you!

CHOOSE ANY PHOTOGRAPH FROM THIS BOOK

for your FREE Mounted Print. Order further prints at half price

Fill in and cut out the voucher on the next page and return it with your remittance for £2.50 for postage, packing and handling to UK addresses (US $5.00 for USA and Canada). For all other overseas addresses include £5.00 post and handling.
Choose any photograph included in this book. Make sure you quote its unique reference number eg. 42365 (it is mentioned after the photograph date. 1890 / 42365). Your SEPIA print will be approx 12" x 8" and mounted in a cream mount with a burgundy rule line (overall size 14" x 11").

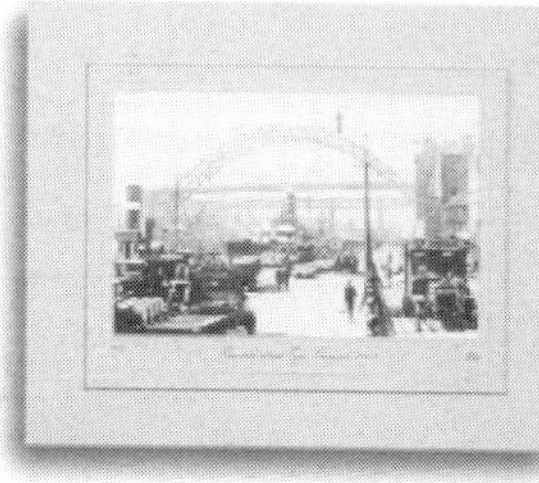

Mounted Print
Overall size 14 x 11 inches

Order additional Mounted Prints at HALF PRICE - If you would like to order more Frith prints from this book, possibly as gifts for friends and family, you can buy them at half price (with no extra postage and handling costs) - only £7.49 each (UK orders), US $14.99 each (USA and Canada).

*** IMPORTANT!**

These special prices are only available if you order at the same time as you order your free mounted print. You must use the ORIGINAL VOUCHER on the facing page (no copies permitted). We can only despatch to one address.

Have your Mounted Prints framed (UK orders only) - For an extra £14.95 per print you can have your mounted print(s) framed in an elegant polished wood and gilt moulding, overall size 16" x 13" (no additional postage).

FRITH PRODUCTS AND SERVICES

All Frith photographs are available for you to buy as framed or mounted prints. From time to time, other illustrated items such as Address Books, Calendars, Table Mats are also available. Already, almost 50,000 Frith archive photographs can be viewed and purchased on the internet through the Frith website.

For more detailed information on Frith companies and products, visit

www.francisfrith.co.uk

For further information, trade, or author enquiries, contact:

The Francis Frith Collection, Frith's Barn, Teffont, Salisbury SP3 5QP

Tel: +44 (0) 1722 716 376 Fax: +44 (0) 1722 716 881 Email: sales@francisfrith.co.uk

Voucher *for FREE and Reduced Price Frith Prints*

Do not photocopy this voucher. Only the original is valid, so please fill it in, cut it out and return it to us with your order.

	Picture ref no	Page number	Qty	Mounted @ £7.49 UK @$14.99 US	Framed + £14.95 (UK only)	US orders Total $	UK orders Total £
1			1	Free of charge*	£	$	£
2				£7.49 ($14.99)	£	$	£
3				£7.49 ($14.99)	£	$	£
4				£7.49 ($14.99)	£	$	£
5				£7.49 ($14.99)	£	$	£
6				£7.49 ($14.99)	£	$	£
	Please allow 28 days for delivery			* Post & handling		$5.00	£2.50
				Total Order Cost	US $		£

Title of this book ....

I enclose a cheque / postal order (UK) for £ .... $ ....
payable to 'Francis Frith Collection' (USA orders 'Frith USA Inc')

OR debit my Mastercard / Visa / Switch (UK) / Amex card / Discover (USA) *(credit cards only on non UK and US orders)*, card details below

Card Number

Issue No (Switch only) Valid from (Amex/Switch)

Expires Signature

Name Mr/Mrs/Ms ....

Address ....

....

....

Postcode/Zip.................... Country ....

Daytime Tel No .... Valid to 31/12/06

PAYMENT CURRENCY: We only accept payment in £ Sterling or US $. If you are ordering **from any other country, please pay by credit card**, and you will be charged in one of these currencies.

Send completed Voucher form to:

UK and rest of world - The Francis Frith Collection, Frith's Barn, Teffont, Salisbury, Wiltshire SP3 5QP England

USA and Canada orders - Frith USA Inc, 11447 Canterberry Lane, Parker, Colorado, 80138 USA

If you need more space, please write your address on a separate sheet of paper.